169 Ways to

SCORE POINTS

with Your

BOSS

Alan R. Schonberg

with Robert L. Shook and Donna G. Estreicher, Ph.D.

CONTEMPORARY BOOKS

Library of Congress Cataloging-in-Publication Data

Schonberg, Alan R.
    169 ways to score points with your boss / Alan R. Schonberg, with
Robert L. Shook and Donna G. Estreicher.
        p.   cm.
    ISBN 0-8092-2998-6 (cloth). — ISBN 0-8092-2999-4 (pbk.)
    1. Managing your boss.   2. Success in business.   3. Supervisors—
United States.   4. Industrial relations—United States.   I. Shook,
Robert L., 1938–   .   II. Estreicher, Donna.   III. Title.
HF5548.83.S36   1998
650.1′3—dc21   97-46456
                                                       CIP

Cover and interior design by Scott Rattray

Published by Contemporary Books
An imprint of NTC/Contemporary Publishing Company
4255 West Touhy Avenue, Lincolnwood (Chicago), Illinois 60646-1975 U.S.A.
Printed in the United States of America
International Standard Book Number: 0-8092-2998-6 (cloth)
                                          0-8092-2999-4 (paper)

18   17   16   15   14   13   12   11   10   9   8   7   6   5   4   3

To my wife, Carole,
and my children, Bill, Lynn, David, and Jeff

Acknowledgments

WRITING THIS BOOK was a team effort, accomplished by scores of dedicated Management Recruiters International (MRI) associates and valued clients. If there was a captain of this team, it was Vince Webb, our multitalented marketing vice president, whose efforts ranged from inspiring MRI associates to contribute their ideas to serving as liaison between MRI and my coauthors, Bob Shook and Donna Estreicher. Vince's invaluable assistant, Karen Bloomfield, was always there, backing us up whenever needed.

My sincerest gratitude goes to the following MRI associates, who contributed many ideas that appear in this book: Robert Adler, Diane Alexander, Jessica Assal, Bill Baker, Cheryl Barry, Ed Beckett, Frank Black, Rich Bolls, Gary Bozza, Rich Bradfield, Dan Breitfeller, Liz Bruns, Jim Burt, Dennis Butler, Jim Cargill, Debra Carroll, Bob Clingan, Judy Collins, Robin Cook, Candy Cooper, Peter Cotton, Howard Couvillon, David Cox, Bart Daly, Jim Deforest, Tom DiDuca, Charlie Dowd, Majorie Forrest, Don Fowler, Pat Gardner, Pam Gilmore, Helen Gleason, Dick Govig, Ed Gridlay, Mike Hardwick, Bill Healy, Jeff Heath, Ellin Irwin, Peter Isenberg, Jim Jacobs, Paul Jardell, Bill Jose, Steve Kendall, Romaine Kleinfeldt, Don Klosterman, Dick Koob, Jeffrey Kristoff, Dan Larson, Carol Lee, Debbie Loudermilk, Diana Mashini, Doug Mendoza, Fred Meyer, Lynne Mowry, Tom Murphy, Budd Naff, Denton Neal, Martin Nicoll, Bob Plecash, Todd Provost, Pam Riddell, John Rothlein, Alan Sapega, Joni Scheps, Ed Schmitt, Clyde Schubert, Barb Seaman, Art Sheehan, Kim Simchak, Jay Sinclair, Steffani Smith, Steve Spencer, Mary Steinmann, Brett Stevens, Linda Strohan, Al Tarquinio, Bob Vierkant, Chris Walhof, Christian Ward, Tom Weider, Jerry West, Ron Whitney, and Wayne Williams.

Kudos to Bob Shook's assistants, Maggie Abel and Stormy Bailey, who spent many hours typing and editing, and then retyping and reediting. A special thank-you goes to Steve Finkel, president of Professional Search Seminars of St. Louis, a mutual friend who introduced me to Bob.

I am also indebted to our literary agent, Al Zuckerman, president of Writers House. He's considered the best in the publishing industry. Thanks also to Susan Schwartz, senior editor, and Julia Anderson, project editor, of Contemporary Books, who did a wonderful job editing the manuscript. Both of these fine women are stars in their own right.

As I said, this was a team effort, and I am very grateful for the contributions made by so many fine individuals.

Alan R. Schonberg

Introduction

As CEO OF THE world's largest search and recruitment firm, MRI, I'm sometimes asked what I think it takes to succeed in a highly competitive job market. My stock answer is "Be sure to get along with your boss."

A little while ago, over dinner with some MRI franchisees and managers, that remark triggered a lively discussion about different ways people score points with their bosses. Some of the comments were so intriguing, I decided to write a book on the subject.

Although I had some thoughts of my own in this area, I wanted to draw upon the expertise of others. For starters, I figured I could pick the brains of some of my company's top people. After all, these professionals have over the years placed more than half a million middle and senior managers with companies in virtually every industry across America.

So I began research for this book by surveying some 3,500 MRI professionals, men and women in constant daily contact with thousands of bosses and job seekers. Then, I surveyed some bosses among our long list of clients—CEOs, senior managers, and human resources vice presidents at thousands of the nation's leading corporations. From these sources sprang this collection of expert opinions from both inside and outside the professional headhunting industry.

While scoring points with your boss has always been a necessity in the workplace, I believe it's more important than ever in today's fast-changing business world. In the modern work environment, you are no longer guaranteed that you'll spend your entire career with the same employer. Over the course of the next 25 to 35 years, you may in fact work for several different companies. Keep in mind that no matter where you work, the odds are high you'll always have a boss—even after you become a boss!

Some people claim that downsizing is the major cause of job insecurity. I refer to it, however, as *rightsizing* because changes in technology require that certain human skills constantly be replaced by other human skills. Individuals who adapt are able to take responsibility for their careers and will always be indispensable to their companies. They guarantee their own job security by continually developing and honing marketable skills that can transfer from one company to another.

As these individuals keep adjusting to an ever-changing work environment, they rely on their people skills to stay in harmony with the boss. They understand that although companies and positions may change over the course of a career, the need to maintain a strong relationship with one's boss remains constant.

It boils down to this: careerwise, your boss is the most important person you have to please. How your boss views you is essential to your career and can even affect your personal life. Your boss's satisfaction with your work and attitude directly influences your present and future job security.

169 Ways to Score Points with Your Boss promises something special for you and your boss because it's filled with field-tested ideas that will make you a better employee. It's not likely that every one of the 169 tips will be applicable to your situation. But then again, you don't need all 169 tips to please your boss—you need only the right ones to do the job. So while you read this book, pick and choose what works best for you. By being selective, you can customize this book to work specifically for you.

I invite you to explore *169 Ways to Score Points with Your Boss* so that you may not only survive but prosper in the new millennium. It's based on the collective wisdom of the country's most knowledgeable career people, bosses, and yes, even the bosses' bosses. I promise you it has something for everyone—in particular, for you and *your* boss!

I. Be Customer Driven

EVERY BUSINESS HAS CUSTOMERS—they are its reason for being. It is in your best interests to strive to understand how your work affects the customer—the end user. Concern for the customer's needs isn't the sole responsibility of the sales force. Whether you are in accounting, the mailroom, or the warehouse, figure out how your job can be fine-tuned to better serve the customer. No matter what your job description says, serving the customer is your job! Only when you fully comprehend how you can increase customer satisfaction will you be able to maximize your performance. Think of the customer as your ultimate boss—for in the final analysis, that's who determines your paycheck!

2. Remember That Time Is Money

WHEN YOU WASTE time during your work hours, your boss pays you money you didn't earn. For example, an employee who comes to work 10 minutes late and leaves 5 minutes early every day is paid for 75 minutes of work that wasn't performed every week. While that might not sound like much, 75 minutes multiplied by 50 weeks comes to 3,750 minutes, or 62.5 hours a year. If the employee earns $20 an hour and works 40 hours a week, that's $1,250 per year in unearned pay. If the employee earns $50 an hour, the yearly total of unearned pay is $3,125. The minutes—and unearned dollars—really add up. No doubt about it, the boss is aware of how much this lost time is costing. Wouldn't you, if the money were coming out of your pocket?

Knowing that time is money, give your boss more than she bargained for. Come to work early and stay a few minutes late every day. If she's one of those people who start very early and work very late, she will likely admire others who do the same. So now and then, show up before she arrives and stay after she leaves.

3. Look the Part

CONTRARY TO THE POPULAR adage, people *do* judge books by their covers. At work, it's important to dress appropriately not only for your current job, but also the job you aspire to. With this in mind, although no written rule states that you have to emulate your boss, you should at least consider dressing compatibly. Why not let your appearance increase your chance for advancement?

Conversely, wearing the wrong outfit can work against you. For the most part, dressing conservatively is the way to go in the business world. Imagine, for instance, the dress code in banking, investments, and the law profession, where a dark suit is more likely to elicit respect and trust. But in industries such as fashion and entertainment, a more contemporary and daring look might be appropriate. No matter the industry, regardless of your personal taste, it's smart to dress the part in your workplace.

4. Read Your Company's Annual Report from Cover to Cover

YOUR COMPANY'S annual report comes out only once a year, and it's rarely more than 40 pages in length. Because it contains a wealth of information about the company, you should read the report cover to cover no matter what your job is. Sadly, most employees—even high-ranked executives—just skim over the annual report, if they even read it at all. By hitting only the highlights, they overlook the detailed explanations appearing in the footnotes. You'll score valuable points with your boss by quoting an obscure tidbit of information he may have skipped. And while you're at it, be sure to read your company's 10K report (the report filed annually with the Securities and Exchange Commission by companies issuing listed securities)—like the annual report, it, too, is public information. By doing this, you never have to discuss important financial data about your company with an outsider who knows more about it than you do.

5. Learn to Handle a Computer

By now, everyone in the workforce should be proficient with computers. This advice applies to everyone from the mailroom employee to the executive vice president. To survive in the 21st century, when the world will be increasingly dependent on computers, you must be computer literate.

Even if your position never requires you to touch a keyboard, failing to understand how these machines work will handicap you. Computer illiteracy will make even the CEO of a large international corporation suffer. Lack of knowledge will make him a weak communicator—out of touch with his people and customers.

6. Be Prepared When You Attend a Meeting

BEFORE ATTENDING a meeting, be sure to do your homework. Read the agenda and all distributed reports and bring them to the meeting so you can actively participate. If additional preparation is required, do it. It's presumptuous to be unprepared, because it causes you to ask others to fill you in on what you should already know. Those who come prepared will rightly feel you have wasted their time. Even if your ignorance is not exposed, you have limited your participation. You're not doing your company a service by sitting there with nothing to contribute. That's no way to please your boss.

By coming to a meeting with your homework done in advance, you can bring thoughtful questions to ask rather than spur-of-the-moment ones. This gives you a tremendous advantage over others who are not as well prepared.

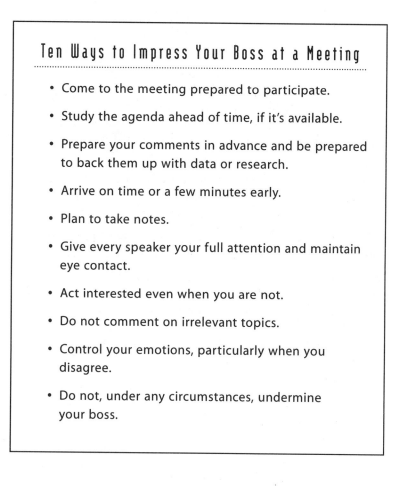

Ten Ways to Impress Your Boss at a Meeting

- Come to the meeting prepared to participate.

- Study the agenda ahead of time, if it's available.

- Prepare your comments in advance and be prepared to back them up with data or research.

- Arrive on time or a few minutes early.

- Plan to take notes.

- Give every speaker your full attention and maintain eye contact.

- Act interested even when you are not.

- Do not comment on irrelevant topics.

- Control your emotions, particularly when you disagree.

- Do not, under any circumstances, undermine your boss.

7. Deliver More than You Promise

ALWAYS DELIVER WHAT you promise. This advice is so basic, it hardly needs mentioning—you probably learned it as a youngster. In the business world, your ability to make and keep promises is one measure of the faith people will have in you and your integrity.

Let's take it one step further. By delivering what you promise, *and then some*, you can really score points. After all, your boss expects you to do what you say you'll do—that's a given. Anything less is poor performance. But star performers go the extra mile—they consistently exceed people's expectations of them. Be one of them, and in time, your reputation for meeting deadlines while still doing work will be so well-established that your boss will rely on you when important tasks need to be done.

Three tips on how to deliver more than you promise:

1. When you are given a quota, don't just meet it— exceed it.

2. Don't simply make a deadline—beat it.

3. Have confidence in your abilities, but be realistic about what you can accomplish. If you bite off more than you can chew, you won't even meet expectations, much less beat them.

One more thing. If you want to stay at your current position, do 100 percent of what your job requires. But if you want to be promoted, do 120 percent of your job! Exemplary performance never goes unnoticed.

SEE ALSO #70.

8. Promote and Use Your Company's Products

It's a sign of good faith to support your company by using its products and services. This lets your boss know you have pride in your work, and it promotes goodwill toward the company among your family, friends, and neighbors. Conversely, it's an insult to your boss and coworkers when you use a competitor's product, like biting the hand that feeds you. Employees who show enthusiasm about their company's products serve as goodwill ambassadors. And by walking in the shoes of the customer, you can remain alert to ideas for needed improvements.

9. Be Prudent with Your Expense Account

WHEN YOUR TAB for travel or entertainment is being picked up by the company, spend your employer's money as frugally as you would your own. First, extravagance is wasteful, and no company wants its employees spending its money foolishly. Second, your boss has probably been around long enough to know what things cost—so assume she's aware of how expense accounts can be padded, and that she wouldn't appreciate it! Third, when you take advantage of an expense account, it signals either that you don't know the value of travel and entertainment, or worse, that you are not trustworthy. And fourth, dishonesty could cost you your job!

10. Be a Good Note Taker

GET IN THE HABIT of taking along a notepad when you meet with your boss. After all, you never know when you will need to capture something significant or lengthy in writing. Whether it's an assignment, a promise, or simply something that ought to be documented for posterity, it's worth taking notes. This sign of your attentiveness will put you in the good graces of your boss. How pleased he will be that you think his pearls of wisdom are worth noting! For the same reasons, you should get in the habit of taking notes when attending committee meetings. Here too, the committee chairperson will be favorably impressed.

II. Never Say Anything Negative About Your Former Company or Boss

CRITICIZING YOUR FORMER company or boss is the kiss of death. No matter how negative your feelings about your last job, keep your thoughts to yourself—especially if you're the new kid on the block. At best, your gripes will sound like sour grapes. At worst, they will paint a picture of someone who has a problem getting along with superiors. Either scenario spells trouble.

When you badmouth an ex-boss, your present boss is bound to wonder how long it will be until you say bad things about her. Such a negative attitude can also signal that you're a troublemaker. Your new boss will think, "There are two sides to every story. I wonder what's really true?" Especially as a new employee, you can't benefit when this kind of doubt is created in your boss's mind. Be careful or you'll be branded as a troublemaker—or worse, find yourself looking for another job.

Six Comments Bound to Turn Off Your Boss

- I've been around here long enough to know it will never work at this company.
- That's not my job.
- Why don't we get off on Presidents' Day?
- I'll do it when I'm through with my coffee break.
- Our church is having a raffle . . .
- Now this is the truth . . .

12. If Your Boss Turns Down Your Suggestion, Don't Take It Personally

NEVER LOSE SIGHT of the fact that your boss has the final say, not you. Even though you may personally think all of your proposals are winners, as the boss, he doesn't have to accept every idea you present to him. Never lose perspective: *he's the boss, and you're not!*

Neither should you take his demurral as personal rejection. The two of you don't have to see eye to eye on every issue, any more than you have to like the same flavor of yogurt. Very likely, your boss is privy to some information that you are not, so what seems like a plausible idea to you might not have the same validity from his vantage point. His insight may be due to confidential information about the company's long-term plan, financial condition, or top priorities—or maybe just a gut feeling based on personal experience.

Whatever it is, you must be thick-skinned enough to understand that it is your boss's prerogative to accept or reject suggestions from subordinates. If you show you are brooding over his decision to overrule you, he'll think you can't handle constructive criticism. You don't want to give him that idea!

Four Smart Questions to Ask Your Boss

- What do you think?
- Is there anything else I should know?
- What would you do first?
- How do you see the end result?

---

13. Make Your Customers Rave About You

CUSTOMER SATISFACTION is a hot buzzword in today's corporate America, and rightfully so. Customers are your company's reason for being, without whom the company would cease to exist. With this in mind, it's no wonder bosses love to hear customers rave about outstanding employees.

There's no secret to getting customers to rave about you. First, never forget that customers always come first. Then, simply give them such incredibly good service that they become customers for life. Customer loyalty results in referrals and repeat business, which builds great companies. In short, it's the backbone of every successful company. Your boss loves to hear glowing reports about you, because they are signs of good business to come! So bend over backward for your customers. Give them a lot of tender loving care.

14. Follow Through

BECAUSE SO FEW people follow through, those who do are deemed exceptional. It's a shame it should be that way, especially in the business world. Everyone—starting with the CEO and including the executive vice president, the sales rep, and the shipping clerk—has a responsibility to follow through with her responsibilities, big and small.

Often, people fail to follow through on small things. When a busy executive doesn't promptly return a phone call or send a thank-you letter to a supplier, a sales rep fails to drop off a promised brochure, or somebody forgets to attend a staff meeting, someone is let down. We all know people who constantly disappoint because they miss deadlines and fail to keep appointments.

The majority of people in the workplace sadly lack follow-through; those who do have it are a rare breed whose dependability is cherished. It's not one big thing, but an accumulation of consistent little things that lets your boss know she can depend on you.

15. Become an Active Member of a Professional Organization

REMAINING CURRENT regarding the latest trends and advancements in your field is a must, no matter how successful you've been. In fact, the more secure you think you are, the more reason there may be for you to become a member of a professional organization. It's an excellent way to avoid complacency.

Don't just join—get involved. Attend seminars and enroll in courses that keep you on the cutting edge. In addition to enrichment from the formal programs you attend at seminars, meeting with your peers from faraway places is an added bonus. Networking and exchanging ideas are side benefits bound to enhance these meetings.

Your commitment to your professional organization reflects well on your professionalism and is certain to please your customers and your boss.

16. Always View Your Job as Important

No matter what your job, you should respect it because it's *yours*. If you project a positive self-image it will be reflected in others' views of you.

When you think about it, even an entry-level employee has an important position—somebody must have thought so or the job wouldn't exist. Under certain circumstances, a low-ranking employee might be more important than a senior vice president on any particular day. Say, for instance, the air-conditioning system goes down on a sizzling-hot summer afternoon. If the maintenance supervisor is the only person in the company who can fix it, he's the man of the hour!

Then too, even routine duties can be performed so that a position takes on a new dimension, far exceeding management expectations. Now and then, highly assertive and creative employees are able to take low-level jobs and turn them into key positions. That's because their performance is so outstanding, their bosses can't help but take notice. These people have figured out how to launch themselves to become their companies' rising stars.

17. Write an Article for Your Company Newsletter

ONE EXCELLENT WAY to get some positive attention within your organization is to be published in its company newsletter. Depending on the nature of the newsletter, your article could range from a report on the progress made by your participation in a quality circle to an in-depth explanation of your research in biochemistry.

Do a professional job. Even if you consider yourself an above-average writer, have someone edit your composition for grammar and content. Seek the help of a friend with good writing and editing skills, or even a professional writer such as a local journalist or English teacher. Don't be too proud to have someone review your writing before submitting it.

It's probable that the article will be read by your boss, your boss's boss, and, in fact, by all your company's VIPs. Need we say more? The people who have the most influence over your career will be reading what you write, so it's important that your writing make a good impression on them.

A well-written article will also be viewed as a feather in your boss's cap, because it makes the entire department look good. Make your boss proud!

18. Take Corporate "Good News" Personally

WHAT IS GOOD for the company is good for you. Those who disagree either have an attitude problem or should change jobs!

Sadly, many employees in corporate America feel detached from the good fortune of their employers. It's as if these employees are saying, "Big deal! What's in it for me?" Such apathy is never appreciated by management.

Let others know that you take great pride in the company's newest client, high production figures, new contract, or improved sales figures. Even though you weren't personally involved in these successes, make it known that you're a loyal member of the team and are delighted by the success of others.

Did you ever notice that even the benchwarmers in the Super Bowl cheer for their teammates to excel? A backup quarterback will root for the team's starting quarterback, even though a successful touchdown drive may keep him out of the game.

Company good news should be welcomed by all employees as a consummation of team performance. Let your sense of pride in your company tell you that a win for the team is *your* win. Be enthusiastic when your company is the recipient of good news—your ebullience will be observed and shared by your boss.

SEE ALSO #76, #88, #96, #128, #137, AND #157.

19. Consider No Task Beneath You

A GOOD LEADER leads by example. By performing menial tasks, you demonstrate to subordinates your willingness to roll up your sleeves and get your hands dirty, sending a message that if you can do it, they can too.

It would be arrogant and pompous to think you're too important to do a seemingly insignificant job. Chances are, your boss isn't above getting her hands dirty either. Surely there are times when she makes her own copies, writes memos on her computer, pitches in to take up the slack for a subordinate—the list goes on and on.

Did you ever notice what happens before a staff meeting gets started when there aren't enough chairs in the room for everyone? While others are standing around twiddling their thumbs, it's generally one of the higher-ranked executives who moves in a few chairs from another office. He's not concerned that anyone will think less of his status, nor does he feel that doing a menial task is an affront to his dignity. What he does want is to get the meeting started without further delay.

Taking the initiative to do a menial task shows your boss that you are a no-nonsense person who takes charge. If you don't take charge with small tasks, why should you be expected to take charge with big tasks? Conversely, people who stand around in a time of need with their noses in the air are demonstrating that they either don't have their priorities straight or lack self-esteem.

20. Praise Others in Public

PRAISING OTHERS is always appropriate in the workplace, but nowhere is it more effective than in the presence of others. Always remember: criticize in private and praise in public. If possible, have an audience assembled when you praise others, especially when commending your boss.

Once you get the hang of it, it's easy to find reasons to offer sincere praise. So don't be shy about dishing it out. And while praise is a tool that superiors can give to subordinates to motivate them, realize that it's a two-way street. Your boss thrives on it just like everyone else.

21. Learn to Work with Less Supervision

BOSSES LIKE EMPLOYEES who can think for themselves. They appreciate individuals who understand an assignment and do it with minimal supervision. Remember that VIPs value their time!

With this in mind, always pay close attention the first time you're asked to do something so you don't have to keep running back to your boss for more instructions. It's OK to ask a lot of questions about your assignment so you clearly understand what you're required to do. But when you're in the middle of a project, take the initiative to do necessary research so you can come up with answers on your own.

Often employees ask the boss to spell out what they are capable of figuring out on their own. Maybe they are insecure about their own judgment, or just crave their boss's attention. In either case, they send a clear signal that they are not capable of taking the ball and running with it. Subordinates unable to think on their feet rarely move up in the ranks. Be a take-charge person, and you'll be tagged as a valuable employee deserving of more responsibility.

SEE ALSO #42 AND #58.

22. Telephone Courtesy with Your Boss

- Never put your boss on hold—take his calls.

- If absolutely necessary, ask your boss if he is able to hold just a moment.

- If he cannot, tell him you will return the call immediately or ask when you may return the call.

- Always return your boss's call as soon as possible.

- Don't have a silly message on your home answering machine that would embarrass you if your boss or an important customer heard it.

23. Get to the Point— Brevity Is a Virtue

LIKE MOST EXECUTIVES, your boss is probably pretty busy. And if you're like many other employees, you probably think you don't get to spend enough quality time with her to express your ideas. Consequently, when you are eyeball to eyeball with her, you may tend to talk too much. As much as you thrive on those private moments with her, respect her time by being brief. The more you drag things out, the less effective you are—and the more she will dread your long-winded narrations.

24. Recognize When a Job Is Finished

EVEN WHEN AN ASSIGNMENT is complete, some people don't know when to stop. Their work is done, but they keep making minor improvements that really aren't worth the extra time they put into it. Instead, they keep mulling over the project, toying with it rather than going on to another assignment in need of their attention. As a result, a disproportionate amount of time is spent changing inconsequential things that make no difference.

It's probable that your boss or your customer won't even detect your added improvement. And it's highly likely they won't appreciate the added expense it cost you to achieve it! Remember, perfection is not a requirement, and in most endeavors, it's not even a possibility.

25. Never Hold a Grudge

No MATTER WHAT has happened, never harbor resentment against anyone with whom you work. Tell yourself that what happened happened, and now it's just water under the bridge. Then forget it and go on with your agenda. There is no place in the office for an emotional outburst, so if you're mad at somebody, just keep it under your hat. Don't allow a grievance to disrupt your work or anyone else's.

This does not suggest, however, that you should ignore being mistreated by others. On the contrary, harboring your feelings is unhealthy and may even invite others to treat you as a doormat. In certain circumstances, you may privately speak to a coworker to explain that you value your relationship with him, and find it necessary to let him know how you feel.

Having employees at each other's throats is not a boss's idea of harmony and teamwork.

26. Go Through the Chain of Command

EVERY ORGANIZATION has a definite hierarchy. To follow the designated chain of command, you must know who all the players are, and how they play. Going over someone's head is a surefire way to alienate a coworker—and the consequences can be even worse when you bypass a superior, especially if it happens to be your boss! Never, absolutely never, go over your boss's head. Such disrespectful behavior shows gross ignorance and is offensive to everyone, including senior management. To many, it's even a sign of disrespect of the system.

Study your company's pecking order—and abide by it. It's there for a purpose. Management didn't draft an organizational chart to be used for wall decoration.

27. Live in the Present

IF YOU ARE NEW in the office, don't turn off your new associates by constantly talking about how your previous company did things. Remember that the former workplace is a thing of the past—you are now part of a new team. Your new company has its own agenda. Drop the old "we" and refer only to your new teammates as "we."

Don't be shy about asking a lot of questions. Not only is it a good way to learn, it demonstrates your interest in your new work as well as your eagerness to learn.

And don't be bashful about jumping right in and getting your feet wet as soon as possible. This, too, shows your new boss and coworkers that you're eager to succeed at your new job. In addition, be willing to share with your new coworkers ideas from your previous work experience. But a word of caution: don't try to impress people with how much you know. Be humble—if you're so smart, they'll find out soon enough.

28. Never Confront Your Boss in the Presence of Others

....

CONFRONTING YOUR BOSS in the presence of others can be lethal to your career. Public confrontations strip away a person's dignity. Not only would such a display embarrass your boss, it would undermine her authority. If you have a conflict with your boss, save it for a private time. Don't allow outsiders to witness strife between you. As Mario Puzo's Don Corleone said to his son Sonny in *The Godfather*, "Santino, never let anyone outside the family know what you are thinking. Never let them know what you have under your fingernails."

SEE ALSO #45 AND #104.

29. Use Flattery Sparingly

WE'VE ALL HEARD the saying "Flattery will get you everywhere," and to a certain extent that's true. But too much flattery can backfire. With this in mind, proceed cautiously when it comes to complimenting your boss. As we all know, even a good thing can be overdone.

Certainly, the strong motivating force of praise is always welcome in the workplace. However, flattery and praise are not synonymous. Praise ceases to be effective when it's laid on so thick that it comes across as phony, reflecting poorly on your sincerity.

Undoubtedly, the biggest drawback in flattering your boss excessively is his eventual recognition that you can't possibly always mean it. Then his appreciation of your sincere praise goes out the window. According to an Italian proverb, "The one who flatters you more than you desire either has deceived you or wishes to deceive." It is not in your best interest for your boss to think this of you.

30. Restaurant Etiquette

- Don't overorder.

- Don't leave the table to greet friends.

- Don't complain about the food.

- Don't order the most expensive item on the menu.

- Express your appreciation when your boss picks up the tab.

- Avoid long conversations on your cellular telephone—better yet, don't take it with you unless absolutely necessary.

- Never talk down to a food server.

- When paying the tab, be a generous tipper.

- Focus on the people at your table—don't let your eyes wander around the room.

- Talk softly—people at other tables have ears and can hear you!

31. Give Only Your Best Ideas

UNLESS YOU'RE IN a long brainstorming session, we recommend that you present your boss with only your best ideas rather than a long series of half-baked ones. Keep in mind that a proposal often is judged by the worst idea in it—at least that's the one someone is most likely to pick on.

It boils down to this: the fewer ideas, the better. The more choices you offer, the greater the chance your boss won't go with the best one. It's a time-consuming task for her to listen to you rattle off dozens of farfetched proposals. Too many suggestions are confusing and tend to delay the decision-making process. Furthermore, by offering too many ideas, you risk presenting a weak one, which will damage your credibility.

When you bring ideas to the table, remember that it's not the quantity but the quality of ideas that counts. Why contaminate your boss's opinion of your good judgment by subjecting her to even one flawed idea?

32. Be a Jack-of-All-Trades

IN TODAY'S HIGHLY competitive workplace, a person with many talents is more apt to survive than is the specialist. With so many companies rightsizing, that is, making staffing adjustments in order to compete in a more efficient workplace, you must develop many skills that heretofore weren't required in order to survive. By possessing many talents, you increase your worth to your company. With technology changing so rapidly, the specialist could find himself obsolete overnight.

Knowing many aspects of your company makes you a more valuable employee. Why? First, it allows you to see the big picture, invisible to the employee who isn't exposed to company activities outside her designated responsibilities. Second, by being a jack-of-all-trades, you are able to pinch-hit when someone, for whatever reason, is not able to do his job. When you have a chance like this to save the day, you'll make a big hit with your boss.

33. Adopt a Lifetime Self-Improvement Plan

As the Red Queen advises Alice in *Through the Looking-Glass*, "Now, *here*, you see, it takes all the running *you* can do, to keep in the same place. If you want to get somewhere else, you must run at least twice as fast as that!" Author Lewis Carroll could have been describing the need in today's business world to adopt a lifetime self-improvement plan. Those who stay in the same place are doomed to become obsolete.

Even after they have achieved success, prominent attorneys, physicians, and educators continue to read journals and attend seminars. Likewise, you must stay abreast of progress in your field. Get into the habit of reading at least 30 minutes a day about your industry. Never rest on your laurels. To move forward, to stay on the top, requires working harder than ever. Successful people don't stop doing the very things that made them successful in the first place.

As part of your lifetime self-improvement plan, you must keep up with changes in your field, exchange ideas with your colleagues, and find better ways to do your job. When you do all of this, your boss is certain to appreciate your desire to advance, and odds are he'll do his best to see that you do.

34. Learn a Second Language

IN TODAY'S SHRINKING world, the need in business to communicate in a foreign tongue is becoming more urgent. No longer is corporate America's marketplace limited to our soil. Speaking another language fluently is an asset not only in dealing with clients and fellow employees, it can be beneficial if you ever accompany your boss to visit with an international client.

Unless you select a very obscure language, you'll probably have many opportunities to exercise your new skills. While French has long been the most popular language for Americans to learn, you might want to consider Japanese, Chinese, or German. Of course, it's wise to base your choice on your company's location and international market. For example, certain parts of the United States have a large Spanish-speaking population. In those areas, learning Spanish would help you converse with customers and employees.

Outside the United States educated people are often bilingual. Chances are that your boss isn't, which is all the more reason for you to be, if you want to impress him!

35. Be a Take-Charge Person

BOSSES LOVE EMPLOYEES who initiate, who take the offensive. Taking charge is a sign of leadership. If you have the stuff that good managers are made of, you will serve as an inspiration to your coworkers and motivate them to follow your lead. One take-charge person can cause an entire team to perform at a higher level. What better way to score points with your boss?

Taking charge signals your boss that you are a self-starter and a leader. When *you make things happen* instead of sitting back and waiting to see what happens, you are a boss's dream!

36. Eagerly Accept Any Offer to Be Compensated on a Performance Basis

As a general rule, most people shy away from jobs that lack a guaranteed fixed salary. They feel that such positions don't offer the security of a steady paycheck and consider working on straight commission risky. But isn't this what all self-employed entrepreneurs do? They have no assurance of a paycheck at the end of the week, or for that matter, at the end of the year. Some may ask, "How can you stand not knowing what your paycheck's going to be?" But some would answer, "How can *you* stand *knowing* what your paycheck is going to be?"

Getting paid for performance is the fairest way to be compensated, because you get paid what you're actually worth. If you perform well, you are paid well; if you perform poorly, you are paid poorly. With this in mind, top producers eagerly welcome an opportunity to be compensated based on performance. And bosses admire the confidence exhibited when an employee bets on her ability and is willing to put everything on the line.

In the long run, your compensation is based on performance no matter how you are paid. Certainly, performing at your highest level will favorably influence your earnings.

37. Eight Things Your Boss Won't Appreciate

- A calendar on your desk marked with the number of days till vacation or retirement

- A copy of *Soldier of Fortune* in your office

- A chain letter to him with your name on it

- Soliciting him to buy something you sell on the side

- Recruiting fellow employees to work for your part-time multilevel marketing organization

- Dressing too casually on casual day

- Using terms of endearment such as "honey" or "dear" in the workplace

- Making excessive personal telephone calls during work hours

38. See the Big Picture, but Pay Attention to Details

Do you remember the riddle "How do you eat an elephant?" The answer is "One bite at a time." In business, while you must see the big picture, paying attention to details is what makes things happen. Too often, we become so focused on a long-term goal that we fail to do the necessary little things along the way. Keep reminding yourself that big projects get done by breaking them down into smaller ones.

As the Chinese say, "The longest journey begins with a single step." A big building is built one brick at a time; a football game is won one play at a time; a book is written one word at a time. Without attention to details, great deeds are never accomplished. While your boss takes delight in your ability to see the big picture, she will quickly become disenchanted if you fail to complete the related day-to-day tasks.

39. Share Your Boss's Priorities

EVERYONE HAS PRIORITIES, especially your boss. Just how well you know and share them is essential to your overall performance. It's important to note that every boss has a distinct set of sacred cows. What was important or even vital to your previous boss may be only a minor concern to your present boss.

For instance, when looking at market share and the bottom line, bosses who think short term are concerned about immediate profits, and those who think long term focus more on the big picture. Or maybe one boss is a stickler for promptness, another for formality, still another for details—the list goes on and on. What matters is that you read your boss and understand his needs and priorities.

40. Subscribe to *The Wall Street Journal*

EVERYONE WORKING IN or aspiring to a managerial position should keep abreast of what's going on in the business world. The best source for such information is *The Wall Street Journal*, so get into the habit of reading it on a regular basis. It's especially important to read it if your boss does too. You're sure to score a few points when she sees a copy on your desk every day!

While you probably won't read every detail, be sure to pay special attention to those articles relating directly to your industry. By checking the paper's index, you can spot articles pertaining to companies in your industry.

SEE ALSO #47, #54, AND #100.

41. Learn from Your Mistakes

It's inevitable that you will make mistakes on the job. Naturally, some will be so minor that nobody but you will notice them. But occasionally, you'll find yourself in the hot seat for a major faux pas.

You must realize that nobody is perfect and that your boss actually expects you to make your share of mistakes. Don't be too proud to admit that you make them—what really counts is how you react to them.

It's been said that the greatest lessons one can learn are those taught by mistakes. Thomas Edison, while inventing the electric light, tried 25,000 times before he finally got it to work. A reporter once asked him, "How did you deal with 25,000 failures?" Edison replied, "I did not fail 25,000 times. I was successful in finding 25,000 ways the light bulb didn't work."

Incidentally, Edison holds the record for most patents granted by the U.S. Patent Office with 1,093 to his credit. Obviously, many of those patents are a result of Edison's sheer tenacity, always searching for new ways to make things work.

As you can see, what others perceived as failure, Edison—the nation's greatest and most prolific inventor—considered feedback. We all make mistakes. Successful people learn and grow from theirs.

42. Ask Questions

THE MORE YOU ASK, the more you know. While some people are embarrassed to ask questions, successful people understand the value of asking thoughtful questions.

It's essential to understand what's expected of you when your boss gives you an assignment. Don't be shy about interrogating her before taking it on. If you leave yourself in the dark by failing to ask the right questions, you'll be operating with a severe handicap because you won't understand what you're expected to do. It's far better to inquire about your assignment in the beginning—that's when your boss expects you to question her.

Sadly, many people are afraid to ask questions because they want to give the impression that they know all the answers. True professionals, however, aggressively ask questions. Did you ever notice, for example, how intently a physician probes a patient's health history before determining appropriate treatment? Likewise, an attorney questions his client before resolving what action to take, and a banker thoroughly investigates customers before agreeing to make loans. Never be embarrassed to ask questions. It's the smart thing to do.

SEE ALSO #21 AND #58.

43. Be Visible

IN A LARGE organization where you don't have daily contact with your boss, it's important for you to maintain a high profile. Make an effort to be noticed on a regular basis.

But be subtle. No grandstanding. First and foremost, perform outstandingly, and chances are your boss will take notice. Sometimes, however, it's also necessary to promote yourself, acting as your own PR agent. When you do something extraordinary, don't be shy about passing the word throughout the organization. Perhaps a call to the editor of the company newsletter is in order. But again, subtlety is the key. You don't want to appear to be blowing your own horn, at least not too loudly. If you have a mentor within the company, drop a hint to him to make sure you get proper recognition for your achievement.

Other ways to create high visibility can range from being a community leader to giving exceptional service to customers. The more raves about you that get back to your boss, the more points you'll score.

44. Keep Yourself in Good Physical Condition

YOU DON'T HAVE to be a professional athlete for your career to benefit from keeping physically fit. The obvious gains of good appearance and added energy enhance any vocation. Impressive appearance provides more than a superficial advantage. People who neglect their physical appearance give the impression that they lack self-discipline, especially when compared to people who watch their diet and regularly work out.

Most certainly, your boss will appreciate your added stamina, particularly at the end of a long day's work. Physically unfit people often tire or lose their sharpness by midday. They are also more prone to illness, and absenteeism is an expense no boss welcomes.

And, as the expression goes, "A good body makes for a sharp mind." This is not just idle chatter, but a medically proven fact. Being physically fit increases your alertness, vitality, and mental responsiveness.

Lastly, and perhaps most importantly, people who work to keep themselves in good physical condition are likely to have a positive self-image. Because they feel and look good, they usually like themselves and exude confidence and energy that attracts others. Your positive self-image will prove contagious as other people, including your boss, share the positive opinion you have of yourself.

45. Never Get into an Argument with Your Boss

It doesn't take a rocket scientist to recognize the futility of arguing with your boss. What chance do you have of winning? It's not that your boss is always right and you're always wrong, but why win a battle and lose the war? Argumentativeness, never an endearing trait, is counterproductive and time consuming and bound to put your boss in a foul mood. Don't be one of those people who always plays the role of the devil's advocate. While it's OK every now and then, if you do it too often it gets annoying! So avoid even the most tempting quarrels. As the expression goes, "Never draw a sword on a king unless you intend to slay him." Be practical. You can't slay your boss!

See also #28 and #104.

46. Don't Try to Impress Your Boss with Constant Conversation

SOME EMPLOYEES TRY too hard to impress the boss by talking incessantly. They think of themselves as a source of information, when in fact they are simply babbling and disrupting the boss's schedule.

During office hours, limit your conversations with the boss to business—and stick to the business at hand. Random chatting, no matter how brilliant, that doesn't contribute to the business of the day is certain to agitate your boss. Rather than accepting your comments as the insightful wisdom they were intended to be, he may view them as mere interruptions.

Repeated attempts to impress your boss could backfire, impressing him negatively. It's better that people wonder why you didn't talk than wonder why you did.

47. Send Your Boss an Occasional News Article

IF YOU READ an interesting newspaper or magazine article related to your business, consider clipping it out to send to your boss in case she missed it. Even if your boss didn't miss the article, she'll appreciate your thoughtfulness and will be impressed that you read it, too.

This is such a thoughtful gesture, you should get in the habit of doing it not only with your boss, but with lots of people—including your customers. It's an expression of your feelings, a way of showing you care about somebody. What a great impression to give your boss!

Throughout the year, this gesture can create even more goodwill than sending a birthday or holiday card. Furthermore, unlike greeting cards, chances are your article is the only one she'll receive that day.

If you decide to do this, be sure to send the original article rather than a copy whenever possible. Include a brief personal note such as, "Thought you'd be interested in this." And don't overdo it. There's such a thing as overkill; if you inundate her with too many clippings, you'll become a nuisance.

SEE ALSO #40 AND #54.

48. Polish Your Writing Skills

NO MATTER WHAT work you do, you must have a basic proficiency in writing if you expect to move up the corporate ladder. Nothing is a bigger turn-off to senior management than an employee whose writing level borders on illiteracy. Yet surprisingly, many would-be candidates for upper-management positions never advance due to weak writing skills. Poorly written memos and correspondence sent to a superior, associate, or customer can be the kiss of death for someone with aspirations for promotion and reflect poorly on your boss.

Imagine a resume that lists a former occupation as "accounting cleric," something entirely different than an accounting *clerk*. Just as such mistakes can deny someone the chance at an interview, so can similar mistakes cost you a raise or a promotion. So do what it takes to brush up on your writing. Enroll in night school or a correspondence course, check out grammar books from the library, or hire a tutor. If you're dispatching memos and letters that embarrass you, take action immediately.

49. Be Loyal to Your Boss

To a certain extent, a boss must earn a subordinate's loyalty. However, as a subordinate, you owe loyalty to your boss, if for no other reason than because he's the person who signs your paycheck.

Unfortunately, in today's fast-moving, mobile society, loyalties don't seem to run as deep as they once did. Nonetheless, loyalty is still an admirable quality, one that gets noticed and rewarded.

Showing loyalty is simple. For one thing, never say anything negative about your boss behind his back. The lesson that you were taught as a child is still appropriate—if you don't have something good to say about someone, don't say anything at all. And when somebody criticizes your boss, stand up for him. Also, when in the presence of others, don't contradict what your boss says, even if you disagree with it. Save your comments for a private discussion.

Bosses are human; they can forgive carelessness, shortcomings, tardiness, and even bad manners. But disloyalty is a true character flaw—it is inexcusable.

50. Practice Common Courtesy with Everyone

To PARAPHRASE A SAYING, be courteous to the people you pass on the way up the corporate ladder, because you never know when you'll meet them on the way back down. This kind of courtesy is more than just good office etiquette. Well-bred and thoughtful people are polite to everyone, no matter what their station in life.

Notice that well-respected top managers treat everyone with equal importance. They extend warm and sincere greetings to all employees, no matter what their position in the company. They don't act as if they are superior to people at the bottom of the corporate ladder. Only the manager with little self-esteem is discourteous to subordinates. Such people are only trying to flaunt their authority.

Your boss will take notice if you treat everyone you encounter with courtesy. This includes everyone from a forgetful flight attendant to an inept repairman. Don't think your boss will be impressed by the way you read the riot act to a waitress who was 20 minutes late with your well-done steak that was ordered rare! When you belittle people, you only make yourself seem small.

51. Realize That the Squeaky Wheel Does Not Always Get the Grease

CONTRARY TO POPULAR belief, the squeaky wheel doesn't necessarily get the grease, especially in the business world. Rather, to paraphrase a Japanese proverb, the nail that sticks up highest gets pounded down the hardest.

Nobody likes a complainer who continually nags until she gets her way. True, some people feel this approach gets the best results—the idea being to wear someone down until he gives in and gives you your way. But, there are more effective ways to influence and win over your boss.

The incessant grumbler is unlikely to become one of the boss's favorites. Whether the complaints are about office matters, government, family members, or just rush hour traffic, endless complaining can get on anyone's nerves, even those of a boss who started out adoring you. Instead of getting a gob of grease, complaints could result in a permanent slide out the front door!

52. Admit Your Mistakes

A MISTAKE IS HARD for some to admit because they feel that to do so is a sign of weakness, an acknowledgment of failure. On the contrary, it takes a strong person to admit a mistake; weak people can't take the heat. Fortunately, good bosses understand this. They know that competent people with high self-esteem are capable of saying, "I was wrong."

In the business world, it's particularly important to be able to fess up to a mistake. To ignore it and hope that it will go away is bound to compound the problem. Better to face up to it immediately and nip the problem in the bud. The longer your wrongdoing goes unnoticed, the more harm it's certain to do. So learn to bite the bullet and minimize your losses. If you wait too long, chances are someone else will reveal your secret, leaving you looking as if you got caught with your hand in the cookie jar. This is exactly why you want to be the one to reveal your error. The worst thing that can happen is for someone else to expose you to the boss. Should that occur, you'll appear as if you either were in the dark about it, or—worse—were trying to cover it up.

In the world of business, where risk taking is common and necessary, everyone will make mistakes sooner or later. And those who never make mistakes are viewed as people who are afraid to take risks.

53. Watch Your Body Language

BODY LANGUAGE reveals a lot about a person's character, particularly her respect for the person she is talking to—or her attentiveness. Follow these guidelines:

- Don't stand too close.

- Don't back someone into a wall.

- Sit attentively in a chair, not slumped.

- Focus on the person you're talking to—don't let your eyes wander around the room.

- Keep your legs still.

- Don't fiddle with your pen, keys, or other objects.

While body language sends a subtle message, it's one that your boss will certainly pick up.

54. Stay Current

"STAY CURRENT" IS another way of saying "Get with it." In today's fast-paced world, you fall behind the times if you become complacent. It's not necessarily age that determines whether you keep up with today's scene. Many of the sharpest people are seniors, and young people can let themselves become old-fashioned in their thinking.

People who are out of touch with what's happening are often viewed as dinosaurs. These dinosaurs are viewed as individuals who resist change—a kiss of death in today's fast-paced, ever-changing marketplace. At all costs, avoid giving the impression that you are a relic out of sync with the times, because then your opinions will hold little value for others. In business, one must look ahead, and someone who can't even stay current is unlikely to be regarded as a visionary.

SEE ALSO #40, #47, AND #100.

55. Accept the Blame, Even When It's Not Your Fault

THERE ARE TIMES when you've got to take the heat even though you're not in error. Sure, nobody likes to be the fall guy, but sometimes that's just the way it is—especially when your boss has backed himself into a corner.

When the boss points the finger at you to cover up for his mistake, you've got to grin and bear it. Hopefully, when things cool down, he'll appreciate you for taking the blame. Of course, you could go at him toe-to-toe, and you might even prove your point. But as the saying goes, you could also end up winning the battle and losing the war.

When you do take the blame, do it quietly. This is not the time to act like a hero. In time, your boss will learn the real truth, and when that day comes, you'll score big-time points with him.

56. Work Overtime

AMBITIOUS PEOPLE emulate the work habits of their superiors. With this in mind, you'll notice that your company's top-ranking managers appear eager to work long hours. Observe the way they come in early and stay late: few top managers limit their schedules to a 40-hour week.

You'll score many points with your boss by demonstrating your willingness to work long hours. After all, what boss isn't interested in getting more bang for her buck! Conversely, it's a real turn-off for a boss to see a subordinate cleaning up his desk 15 minutes before quitting time and making a beeline toward the door as the time nears 5 o'clock. This sort of behavior sends a definite message to management that the employee lacks enthusiasm and commitment.

When your boss sees you putting in extra hours on your own time, he appreciates that you are making personal sacrifices to lend a hand. You don't even have to mention what you're doing because your actions clearly demonstrate your loyalty to the company and your commitment to your job. People who make a big fuss over any extra time they put in end up annoying their bosses with their obvious attempts at self-promotion.

Don't cancel out the points you score working overtime by complaining about all the things you're missing out on. The more you express your exasperation, the more fed up your boss will get. If you protest too much, your boss won't even appreciate that you worked the extra hours, and instead of scoring points you'll actually lose points. What a pity, because all of your hard work will have been in vain.

If you're a recently hired college graduate, you especially should demonstrate a willingness to work long hours, and by doing so prove to your boss that what you may lack in experience you are eager to make up for with hard work and desire. Let's face it—as an inexperienced new recruit in training, your contribution at first will be minimal. So when you work overtime, your enthusiastic attitude will make a statement that you're willing to make sure your company gets its money's worth.

See also #144.

57. Be a Good Sport and Occasionally Pick Up the Tab

WANT TO REALLY make an impression on your boss? Pick up the check the next time you're eating out with him on a nonbusiness occasion.

Just as you wouldn't let a close friend always get stuck with the tab, neither should you take for granted that meals are always the boss's treat. It's simply not in good taste to let somebody—even a boss—continually pick up the check. Many employees think dining out with the boss means an automatic free meal and take the privilege for granted.

You don't have to do it all the time, and it doesn't have to be on an equal basis, but every now and then, make an honest attempt to reach out for the check when the server puts it on the table. If your boss politely resists, next time make arrangements with the server before the meal. And one more thing—*never* invite your boss to lunch for a special occasion (for example, her birthday) and let her pick up the tab!

58. Don't Fake It—Be Sure You Understand the Assignment

DON'T SUBSCRIBE to the fake-it-until-you-make-it philosophy, and don't be afraid to speak out when you don't understand an assignment. It's much better to ask questions up front rather than remain silent and fail to meet your boss's expectations.

By pretending you understand an assignment when you really don't, you risk going off in the wrong direction when a quick inquiry could have put you on the right track. Not only does asking questions save *you* time and energy, it saves your company—and your boss—time, energy, and company money! Depending on how long the assignment takes, a few moments of extra instruction can save hours or days of wasted time and energy. In this respect, remaining silent to save face is more than false pride—it's cheating the person who pays your salary.

SEE ALSO #21 AND #42.

59. Put Yourself in Your Boss's Shoes

MOST OF US KNOW how to apply the adage about walking a mile in another's moccasins. Generally, it is applied in situations where we have empathy for somebody in a lower position than ours. Hence, it's more appropriate for your boss to put himself in your shoes than vice versa.

But on occasion, put yourself in your boss's shoes so you can see things from his vantage point. Ask yourself, "What would I do if I were in charge?" Imagine yourself sitting behind his desk and trying to make decisions. Your perspective will change quickly!

As the saying goes, it's lonely at the top. By putting yourself in the boss's shoes, you'll discover that he must frequently struggle to make hard decisions and balance the needs of the employees and the profitability of the company.

60. Send Your Boss a Complimentary Memo

HERE'S A TIP WITH a twist: send your boss a memo telling her what a good job she's doing. Good bosses routinely give this kind of encouragement to their subordinates, and such a note from the top is always well-received. In fact, it usually makes the recipient's day. And like the rest of us, bosses appreciate praise and a pat on the back.

Of course, when you do this, it must be a sincere compliment, otherwise it will be viewed as buttering up the boss, which will have a negative effect. But if you're the kind of person who normally compliments people, this should come naturally to you. You shouldn't deny your boss this courtesy simply because she's your boss. In fact, when it comes to dishing out praise, your boss should be high on your list. Why? Because it's usually more important that your boss think highly of you than do other people.

While a face-to-face compliment is perfectly OK, every now and then do it with a brief memo. This is a nice added touch because it is something your boss can keep and read again when she needs encouragement.

61. If You Can't Say Something Nice About Someone, Don't Say Anything

....

YOUR MOTHER PROBABLY gave you this advice when you were little, and if she didn't, she should have. But sadly, as we get older, we tend to forget to practice it.

In the world of business, badmouthing people goes beyond demonstrating bad manners—you can get canned for it! Or, at the very least, you may get passed over when it's time to hand out promotions. A vocally critical person gets quickly branded as somebody who doesn't have the sense to keep quiet—a trait that's not likely to win anyone's respect for many obvious reasons. What's more, if your boss hears you badmouthing your coworkers, he's likely to suspect you'll do the same thing about him behind his back. In addition, management will make certain you aren't exposed to confidential information that you might reveal to outside sources.

Badmouthing people erodes teamwork because it creates animosity, and this over time pits people against each other. Hence, it creates an environment that's not conducive to a harmonious workforce.

62. Keep Your Private Life Private

DON'T TAKE YOUR personal problems to work with you—they're nobody's business. When people ask, "How are you?" they don't really want to know. They don't care that your father was laid off last week, your furnace broke down, or your ex-wife has filed for an increase in child support payments. So don't burden your co-workers or boss with your personal hardships. Telling them only creates a negative atmosphere that can't possibly do you any good.

There is still another good reason for keeping your personal problems to yourself. If given a choice, you want people to think of you as a pillar of strength, not a pile of misfortunes. Letting coworkers know about your off-the-job struggles is not the kind of personal image you want to project.

Don't delude yourself into thinking you're the only one with personal problems. Everyone has them. Wise people, however, keep them to themselves. When you arrive at the office, there's a business that must operate, and people are busy at their jobs. Discussing your personal affairs with them—even the positive things in your life—is not appropriate on company time. And it's a sure bet your boss isn't going to like it. Why should she when you're distracting people on her payroll from doing their work?

Your good fortunes—your son's Little League hat trick or the fabulous dinner party you attended on Saturday night—shouldn't be discussed either. They may be viewed as boasting and could become the source of envy to coworkers. So even the wonderful things going on in your personal life should be kept private.

A good rule of thumb is to keep your conversations restricted to business during office hours. On your own time you can be more relaxed and socialize with coworkers. Unless you're talking to someone whom you consider a close friend, don't reveal too much about your private life.

63. Accept Criticism Graciously

IN GENERAL, WHEN your boss criticizes you, it's justifiable. Most likely, you haven't performed your work satisfactorily. Assuming you work for a reasonable person, when your boss complains, she isn't on the warpath or out to make your life miserable. Instead, she wants to help you improve your performance. The first thing to keep in mind is that she's doing it with good intentions—so don't be offended.

Handling criticism is a skill worth learning, especially when it's your boss dishing it out. What you don't want to do is to respond in anger. Acting defensively will just make her more uncomfortable than she already is, and possibly even angry. Of course, you have to acknowledge your boss's criticism, but that doesn't mean you must respond immediately. It's perfectly acceptable to delay your response by saying, "I hear what you are saying. If you don't mind, I'd like to give it some thought and get back to you in the morning." By doing this, you present yourself as somebody who is willing to listen, and equally important, willing to learn from your mistake.

Likewise, being thin-skinned sends a signal that you're insecure and think so little of yourself that you can't take not getting your way. You should never take criticism personally. Your boss is not attacking you for what you did. It's not a personal issue, so don't react as if it's personal.

The best way to react is to accept criticism positively and actually thank your boss for it. Say something to her such as, "I truly appreciate your interest in my work, and I will do my best to improve. Thank you for bringing this to my attention." This is not a typical reaction to criticism, and your boss will admire you for such a mature response. This is a prime example of how to turn a minus into a plus!

64. Learn to Read Your Boss's Moods and Recognize That Timing Is Essential

AFTER YOU'VE worked for your boss for some time, you should begin to read his moods. In time, you'll know when you should or should not approach him to discuss such things as a promotion, a raise, or one of your pet projects. The following scenarios are examples of when to keep your distance:

- He's running late for a meeting or other appointment

- He's behind schedule and working overtime to finish a rush project

- He's preparing to deliver an important speech

- He just got chewed out by his boss, a customer, or someone else

- His secretary just quit

- He just had a heated argument with someone

- It's income tax time and his CPA just walked out the door

- He's getting ready to go on vacation

- He just got back from vacation

- It's one of those holiday weeks where everything that's normally done in five days must be squeezed into three days

Get the picture? Undoubtedly, there are many more you can add to this list!

SEE ALSO #136.

65. Get in the Habit of Saying "We" Instead of "I"

WHEN YOU SAY "I have a problem," your coworkers or boss might respond, "I'm busy right now—could we talk about it tomorrow?" But when you say, "We have a problem," you immediately touch a sensitive nerve in people and get their attention. And you've personalized the problem—it becomes their problem, too.

When you talk about company success, using the singular first person sounds egotistical—it's as if you're personally taking credit for what is a team effort. A good team player always emphasizes *we* in addressing or speaking about other team members. This is common even when she actually deserves full credit for her personal achievement. Never hesitate to share credit for your successes with others out of fear you won't be acknowledged for your work. Not only will you receive the recognition you deserve, you'll score extra points for your team spirit and humility.

Another time to use "we" instead of "I" is when you introduce a new idea and want the support of others. By making the idea their idea in the beginning stages, you invite them to participate in it, improve it, and then work to implement it. To paraphrase an old saying, people will support those projects they helped to create. Conversely, if they're not a part of its creation, they will resist it. This is particularly true when it comes to getting them to accept change.

66. Have a Passion for Your Job

DO A QUICK STUDY on the most successful people you know—you'll notice that a common denominator they share is passion for their work. Because these high achievers truly love what they're doing, they are highly motivated, and it's reflected in their productivity.

When you have passion for your work, an unexplainable abundance of energy enables you to put in long hours. This positive attitude is a far cry from the way you feel when working at something you dread. Working at a job you can't stand actually drains your energy, and the related stress can be harmful to your health.

As William Faulkner once wrote, "You can't eat for eight hours a day nor drink for eight hours a day nor make love for eight hours a day—all you can do for eight hours a day is work. Which is the reason why man makes himself and everybody else so miserable and unhappy." Faulkner had the right idea. Since you're going to spend eight hours of your day working, it should be working at something that you'd rather be doing than anything else. People who enjoy their work are the luckiest people in the world.

Because enthusiasm is contagious, having a passion for your work inspires others to rally around you. This includes your boss. In time, she'll become one of your most ardent supporters.

67. Seek a Mentor Your Boss Respects

WHEN IT COMES to choosing the right mentor, it goes without saying that you want a person who is accessible and can properly advise you. Another important criterion is that the mentor be someone your boss respects. If your boss is impressed with this person, he'll also respect your actions that are based on the mentor's advice.

With this in mind, seek out a mentor in a high position—if possible, equal to or above your boss's position. If you do this, your boss is more likely to be influenced by the advice you carry out. And if you're really in tight with your mentor, who knows, your boss may even try to score points with you to get in good with the mentor!

Of course, if you don't land a mentor you think your boss respects, you might get your boss to be your mentor. Get him to tell you about how he climbed the corporate ladder when he was just starting his career. Generally, a boss enjoys sharing the tale of his way upward, so listen carefully. Meanwhile, you'll be privy to some good clues that will apprise you of what he admires in someone eager to advance.

68. Learn to Work Around Your Boss's Idiosyncrasies

LIKE THE REST of us, your boss undoubtedly has her share of quirks and hang-ups. If you haven't noticed them yet, give her time. It's a safe bet that you'll soon discover a few. After all, she's human like the rest of us.

Naturally, you have a choice. You can let her idiosyncrasies drive you up the wall, or you can learn to live with them. If you allow them to get to you, you'll only make yourself frustrated. Recognize that she's not about to let go of her quirks, any more than you're about to let go of yours. So be adaptable and accept her flaws with a grain of salt. For instance, rather than blowing a gasket every time she goes bananas when you don't answer the phone before the fourth ring or when she starts to foam at the mouth because you're running behind schedule for a meeting, do what you must do to keep her blood pressure down.

It's a rare thing when people rid themselves of an idiosyncrasy, so instead of hoping for a miracle, accept your boss as is. She's stuck with her ways, and at work, you're stuck with her!

69. Pay Close Attention to Your Company's Unwritten Rules

EVERY ORGANIZATION has dozens of decrees deeply embedded in its culture that never appear in writing. Just how these unwritten rules started may or may not be clear, but just the same, everyone in the company who doesn't want to make waves obeys them. Similarly, your company may even have written rules that no one abides by. What matters, however, is that you are observant enough to know which rules are important—and never deviate from them.

Just what are a few of these unwritten rules? One may be that a telephone must always be answered by the fourth ring, another that everybody calls the boss by his first name. Maybe a customer should always be greeted in a particular way, for example, "Good afternoon, sir, may I help you?" Some of these are trivial, but others are sacred in the corporate culture.

One of the most famous unwritten rules was IBM's dress code, which for many years assured that every employee who called on customers wore a dark conservative suit, white shirt, and quiet tie. While this dress code never formally appeared in writing, to IBM employees, it was engraved in stone. IBM's dress code was in effect for several decades, and employees were not permitted to dress more casually until the mid-1990s.

70. Seek Increased Responsibility

To ADVANCE IN the corporate world, it's not enough to simply do what's expected of you. In today's highly competitive workplace, just getting by won't cut it. Not only must you take everything your boss sends your way, you must take aggressive steps to increase your responsibilities.

This means that in addition to handling your normal workload, you must volunteer for extra assignments. And if your boss doesn't have anything extra for you, then you must create supplementary responsibilities. You might offer to help train a new employee. This is typically a task that no boss welcomes, but somebody has to do it—so you volunteer and you're bound to score some extra points.

The average employee will shake her head and say, "Why volunteer for extra work? That's crazy." But remember, the average employee doesn't really want to climb the corporate ladder, she only wants to dream about it. You're different because you'll pay the price to make it happen. It's not easy, but anything worthwhile rarely is.

SEE ALSO #7.

71. If a Joke Is Not Funny and Not Offensive, Laugh Anyway

SOMETIMES IT'S EASY to add a little happiness to another person's life. All it takes is for you to laugh at a joke he tells—even if it's not funny or it's one you've already heard. For what it's worth, you can view this as an act of charity.

If you can't muster up a laugh, even a warm smile or small grin will do. It requires no effort on your part. But sitting there with a straight face after someone has told a joke—well, that's just not nice! If you've ever told a quip that cracked you up but didn't provoke even the slightest titter, you know the awkward feeling that follows the long, seemingly endless silence of a bombed joke. An unpleasant and cumbersome moment of this nature isn't what you want to inflict upon your boss.

Remember too, that when your boss tells you a joke, he obviously thinks it's funny or he wouldn't be telling it. When you don't react to what he thinks is clever, witty, or hysterical, he may surmise two things that could, indeed, subtract points from those you already have accumulated: you are dull and humorless, or you have a sense of humor but are just too slow to get it!

72. Make Business Lunches Productive

DURING A BUSINESS lunch, people tend to waste a lot of precious time chit-chatting when they are first seated, and, as a consequence, they don't leave enough time for discussing business at the end of the meal. Many times, that's because they feel uncomfortable talking business in the relaxed atmosphere of a restaurant or dining room. So instead, they socialize and make small talk.

A seasoned businessperson, however, has sat through enough unproductive business lunches. She recognizes very well the importance of conserving precious time by launching a discussion of important matters before the meal. She remains mindful of the rush that can occur at the end of the lunch hour when executives and managers depart to keep other commitments. So to get the ball rolling, she distributes a written agenda prior to the commencement of the luncheon. Knowing that a disproportionate amount of time is generally spent on the food selection from the menu, she might order meals in advance, or at the very least suggest that everyone order as soon as the menu is presented. Speeding up this process not only conserves time, it sets the tone for a productive, no-nonsense business meeting during the meal.

73. Be Sure to Attend Your Boss's Big Speech

IF POSSIBLE, DEPENDING on the location and the time, make an effort to be present when your boss makes an important speech. If he's routinely asked to speak in public, it's not mandatory for you to be there; this advice is more applicable to his once-in-a-blue-moon speaking engagement, the kind that he prepares for weeks in advance and that appears to cause him a bit of anxiety as the date approaches. If it's one of these occasions, chances are he'll appreciate a friendly face supporting him in the audience.

You might even volunteer to listen to him deliver his speech to you as a trial run. If so, offer him encouragement as well as a few tips on his delivery or content. Whatever help you can give him before he speaks will be appreciated.

After the speech, find something to sincerely praise about it, even if you have to search for an area where he excelled. In the event that he bombs, there's no point in telling him after the fact. Your boss knows how it went over. Either way, he'll appreciate a few words of encouragement. If he was so terrible that there's no way you can convince him otherwise, simply reassure him that people appreciate him for his strengths (specify a few) and no one expects him to be a professional speaker.

74. When a VIP Enters the Room, Stand Up to Shake Hands

FOR CENTURIES, standing up has indicated respect when acknowledging a VIP. Get in the habit of doing this, whether you're a man or woman, even if you're the only one who does. Beyond good manners, it's a form of protocol practiced all over the world.

Don't just reserve standing for VIPs—do it when an elderly person enters the room. Sure, some people will view you as being old-fashioned—but politeness and respect for others have never gone out of style—and let's hope they never do.

75. Take a Stand When Necessary

YOU SHOULD ALWAYS be supportive of your boss—if for no other reason, because she is your boss. This does not imply that you should be a "yes-person" when you know she's wrong. Most often, however, it's probable that you and she think alike on most issues, unless the two of you are totally incompatible. (If so, consider a job change.) So let's assume your boss earned the position she's in because she knows what she's doing. This means that in most instances you should be in agreement.

With this said, you still won't be much good to your boss if you never disagree with her. What's more, if you always go along with her she'll soon stop asking your opinion because it never differs from her own. As many CEOs have said, "I have no need for an executive who thinks exactly like I do." A good boss wants to be confronted by subordinates, especially those who offer alternatives. She knows she's not right 100 percent of the time.

What's really important to your boss as well as your coworkers is that you take a stand on what you believe in. While life has a place for compromise, when it comes to principles, you must have conviction. As Thomas Jefferson said, "In matters of principle, stand like a rock; in matters of taste, swim with the current." Those who never stand up for their beliefs are viewed as weak.

SEE ALSO #112.

76. Have a Clear Understanding of Your Company's Values

JUST AS PEOPLE have values, so do companies. Sometimes these values are clearly defined—you'll find them written in mission statements and company newsletters, plastered on posters, and hung as plaques in reception areas and executive offices. They may be referred to as "the bedrocks," "the basic beliefs," and so on. Other times, a company's values are spoken—and practiced—but don't appear in writing—this is how most small companies operate, practicing very basic rules like "The customer is always right," "We stand behind our product," "Strive for excellence," and so on. In time, it doesn't matter what management claims its values are, it's what it does that matters. As Ralph Waldo Emerson put it, "What you are . . . thunders, for I cannot hear what you say." Beware of the company that only gives lip service when it speaks of its values.

With or without the benefit of written documentation, you must identify what your company stands for, and be sure that you share the same values. These values are so important that all major decisions made by management should reflect them. Knowing their influence, if you don't agree with them, you should, in good conscience, find another job.

Remember too, that while everything is subject to change, a company's core values never change. Organizations that truly live by them say that their values are their only sacred cow.

SEE ALSO #18, #88, #96, #128, #137, AND #157.

77. Be a Team Player

TEAMWORK HAS long been a buzzword in the world of business. By now everyone must surely know that a certain synergy results when people work together as a team. In other words, an organization gets more done when its people work in harmony toward a common goal, rather than when each person pulls helter-skelter in a different direction. The objective is attaining the goal, not taking credit for getting there.

In a team, each person does a certain job according to that member's given assignment or special skill. It's easy to see why this approach gets more accomplished, but all too often people resist working as team players. Sometimes an individual is too focused on a personal agenda, or a big ego can stand in the way. Someone may be more interested in attaining personal success than doing what's best for the team. To use a sports analogy, the team with the highest score wins the Super Bowl, not the player who scores the most points.

Of course, a primary function of management is to manage people to work as a team. So for obvious reasons, it's your boss who is best served when you work as a team player!

Bosses like employees who have team spirit. These dedicated workers set high standards for others to follow. And their enthusiasm is contagious—soon it spreads to the entire team. No wonder their bosses love them!

78. Be Coachable

CLOSELY RELATED to being a good team player is allowing your-self to be coached. In sports, star athletes who resist taking orders from the coach are a detriment to the entire team. Good coaches either bench such players or kick them off the team!

In the business arena, being coachable means more than fol-lowing orders—it also means being willing to learn and grow. There's no place in a well-managed organization for employees who think they've reached a point in their careers where it's unneces-sary for them to develop additional skills or improve their work.

Generally, employees who begin their careers at entry-level positions are not brought into the organization for what they know, but instead, for their potential to learn—for what they will eventually know. Nothing pleases a boss more than an enthusias-tic employee, eager to grow and prove her worth to the company. Conversely, those who are unwilling to grow are viewed either as mavericks or deadwood. Today in the ever-changing marketplace, management places a high priority on keeping its people current. This is best achieved with people who are coachable.

Six Tips on Being Coachable

- Always have a burning desire to learn.

- Give your boss credit for knowing his job.

- Don't second-guess your superiors.

- Ask plenty of questions.

- Be a good listener.

- Be flexible.

79. Understand That Life Isn't Fair

JUST IN CASE YOU haven't figured it out by now, life isn't fair. So don't expect the business world to exude a sense of fair play, either. The workplace isn't a game where everyone is given an equal chance to win, nor is business a democracy. So if you're under the impression that working in the free enterprise system means you'll be treated fairly, you're misinformed.

It doesn't matter that you play by the rules, because rules can always be broken, and sometimes there are no rules. Somebody less deserving than you may get the promotion you deserve—it could be the boss's son or niece who gets the job you think should have gone to you.

Many things in business happen that are beyond your control. Although you did your job brilliantly, your department lost money, so your annual bonus is reduced or eliminated. Or worse, the company is shutting down the entire department and suddenly you're unemployed. Or if your company is unable to hold its own with the competition, your future may be bleak just because the company's future is bleak.

The important lesson to be learned is that over the course of time, everyone encounters unfair situations. Unfortunately, some people seem to run into more than their share. Recognize that there are no entitlements in the workplace. When something unfair happens to you, and it will, don't take it personally or make a bigger deal out of it than it really is. Be strong and accept it. How you cope with your disappointment with being treated unfairly is what matters. When your boss observes that you are able to handle disappointment, he will see it as a positive sign, because strong people don't let setbacks defeat them.

80. Get a Life (After Work)

ALL WORK AND NO play does make Jack a dull boy. It can also make Jack a dull executive. In today's competitive workplace, key employees must be well-rounded, and this requires you to have balance in your life. Always remember, there is a time to work and a time to play.

Getting off the work treadmill necessitates unlearning adult competitive goal-oriented behavior. This means relaxing into the healing process of play. It's a proven fact that the mental processes used in play and creative activities change the chemistry of the brain, which, in turn, creates more energy. Play is not a time waster, but a time saver. When you set aside time for play, you're more relaxed, rested, and rejuvenated. In turn, your mind will be more creative and open. This will result in a healthier, more positive attitude. You will discover new solutions and be more likely to view problems as opportunities. As an added bonus, you'll have fewer physical symptoms of colds, headaches, stomachaches, and pains. Consequently, you'll lose less time from work due to illness.

Get your priorities straight. Work is a means to provide for your loved ones and be able to spend quality time with them. If you get too caught up in your work, you could end up neglecting them, and that's not good for them, you, or your company. Should this happen, you could also work yourself into a state of depression, which will serve no useful purpose at home or at the office.

Ten Executive Play Tips

- Take a walk during your lunchbreak or make a quick visit to a favorite store just to browse.

- Rise early and enjoy a brisk walk or jog.

- Eat a healthy lunch away from the office.

- Join a health club; enjoy a regular massage.

- Take the weekend off for a quick getaway.

- Call an old friend.

- Drive a different route home and enjoy the scenery.

- Go to a favorite or new restaurant.

- Enjoy a movie or cuddle up with a good book you've been wanting to read.

- Go to a museum or a concert.

81. Be a Good Backup Person for Your Boss

IF YOU CAN BECOME your boss's number one backup person, you'll soon be an indispensable employee. This will require you to take on added chores—perhaps some of the workload your boss is getting paid a hefty salary to do herself. But if you roll up your sleeves often enough, your boss will become so dependent on you that soon she won't know how to get along without you.

To position yourself for this role, you'll need to think of yourself as a pinch-hitter. Be the one who takes the initiative to cover for her when she's not available. This may be risky, because at times you may find you need to act on your own, even when both you and she might not feel you are ready.

Being a good backup person also means sticking your neck out for your boss when she's not there to defend herself. This blind loyalty is certain to win her admiration and support.

82. Don't Just Complain— Offer Solutions

NOBODY LIKES TO listen to a person who complains about what's wrong but never has solutions. Not only is this behavior annoying, it's unproductive and demoralizing.

When you run to your boss to voice a criticism, chances are you're telling him something he already knows. He doesn't need you to identify problems—he needs you to offer solutions. For example, a salesperson who points out to his boss that the company's prices are too high should then follow up with documentation of the competition's prices and research showing how a price reduction could increase the company's revenues.

An employee who is always pointing out problems without offering solutions is tagged as a negative person. For example, take the individual who comes to committee meetings only to voice what's wrong with everything. No wonder that behind her back, other committee members say, "Oh, there she goes again, finding fault with everyone's ideas. Doesn't she ever have anything positive to add?" You've seen this type at meetings—the individual who takes up a lot of time but rarely contributes anything constructive.

Not that you shouldn't identify a problem when you spot one. That's fine—but after you state it, follow up with some practical ideas on how to solve it. If you do, you will be viewed as an esteemed employee.

83. Ask for Periodic Performance Reviews

BY WAITING UNTIL the end of the year for a job evaluation, you risk being informed that you have performed unsatisfactorily—and then it's too late to do anything about it! Instead, your performance should be reviewed periodically so that if you're doing poorly, you have an opportunity to fix what's wrong.

Depending on the nature of the assignment and its length of time, it's a good idea to meet at regular intervals with your boss to get some feedback about your progress. If you meet early on and you're going in the wrong direction, it's considerably easier to be put back on track during the budding stages of an assignment rather than during the latter stages.

Document your results during the year. This way, when the time comes for a job evaluation, you'll be able to quantify your progress and achievements.

A word of caution: when you meet with your boss for a periodic performance review, don't be thin-skinned about any constructive criticism you receive. Remember that an important purpose of the boss's critique is for you to learn what you need to know in order to excel at your job. Fix whatever your boss says needs to be fixed. You don't want her to be upset the next time around because you're still doing things the old way.

84. Motivate the Motivator

....

WHO MOTIVATES THE motivator? Always remember, bosses are human, too. And from time to time they, like everyone else, need someone to motivate them. Employees tend to forget that the one at the top needs encouragement, too. Bosses have their share of bad days as we all do.

As the saying goes, it sometimes gets lonely at the top. That's because when the going gets really tough, the boss may not have anyone to turn to upstairs. And rarely does she have anyone to reassure her that she's doing the right thing.

After you've worked with your boss for awhile, you should be able to sense her mood swings, so when you see that she needs a few words of encouragement or a pat on the back, don't be shy about trying to lift her spirits. Or when you see that she's suffered a major setback, let her know you're behind her 100 percent. Say something to her such as, "I know you're disappointed, but I want you to know I think you did the right thing and I commend you for it." Or, "Like you have always told me, 'The only people who never make mistakes are those who never take any risks.'" When you say a few encouraging words at the appropriate time, your boss will cherish you for your thoughtfulness.

By stepping into the role as the motivator of the motivator, you become an invaluable asset to your boss.

85. Control Your Anger

OBVIOUSLY THE WORKSITE is not the place to express your anger. But what should you do? After all, if unexpressed anger isn't healthy, then it would be harmful to suppress hostility. The following are eight tips to help you control your anger:

- Pin down the cause of your angry reaction.

- Rather than react impulsively, think about what you want to say to the person who angered you (if anything).

- Allow yourself an adequate cooling-down period before you approach the person who angered you.

- Clearly identify those situations that cause your blood to boil.

- Be alert to symptoms of anger such as tense, tight muscles, speaking in a raised voice, knots in your stomach, quick breathing, increased heart rate, and nervous mannerisms.

- Recognize whether you are reacting to the person who angered you or perhaps some other personal reaction is being triggered.

- Recognize your own mood. Are you tired? Have you been eating properly?

- Offer a constructive solution.

86. Never Ask Your Boss Tough Questions During an Important Presentation— Unless You Know He Can Answer Them

DON'T TRY TO impress everyone by asking a speaker tough questions he might not be able to answer—especially if he happens to be your boss!

It boils down to this: do you want to make your boss look good or look bad in the presence of others? If you ask him difficult questions that come as a surprise during an important presentation, you risk putting him on the spot. To play it safe, be certain he knows the answers. If you're not sure, simply don't ask any questions.

A good trial attorney never asks a question of a witness without knowing how it will be answered. The attorney doesn't want any surprises that can go against her case. Similarly, don't put your boss in the hot seat with a question he might not be able to answer.

87. Seek Simplicity

IN AN ENVIRONMENT where many people are trying hard to impress everyone else, there's a lot to be said for those who embrace simplicity. It's a welcome relief to come across an individual who makes her case plainly and clearly without trying to impress others with how much she knows. You know the type—the person who uses technical terms, acronyms, and jargon in an attempt to appear more knowledgeable than anyone else in the room. If, for example, a doctor were to use complex medical terms to explain common illnesses to his patients, not only would they not understand what he was saying, they might even suffer an anxiety attack!

What does all of the above have to do with scoring points with your boss? A lot. Simplicity relieves stress, and when you're stress free, your work will be positively affected.

As they say in the writing profession, it's hard to write in a style that's easy to read. Sure, a writer could use a vocabulary that's too difficult for the average reader, concentrating on the least recognized words in a thesaurus, but isn't that missing the point? After all, writing is a form of communication—which means that if a writer fails to communicate with the reader, she is failing as a writer.

Likewise, in the workplace the uncomplicated is generally superior to the complicated. Former president Ronald Reagan was a prime example of a speaker who was able to present complex matters in a simplified way—and this skill earned him a reputation as a great communicator.

SEE ALSO #139.

88. Make a Generous Donation During Your Company's United Way Fund-Raising Drive

As THE SAGES once said, "The giving of charity increases one's wealth, and he who refrains from giving hurts himself." Naturally, charity comes from within—you must want to give. And you'll find few better vehicles than the United Way. Of course, you should understand that there are many charities. United Way, however, typifies an all-engrossing charity. It supports many worthy causes and is strongly supported in corporate America.

If you want to score big points with your boss, volunteer for your company's United Way drive. If you really want to impress, volunteer to chair the drive. This requires your commitment to a lot of time and hard work. Achieving these goals will garner you high esteem from management throughout the company.

Many companies pressure middle and senior managers to give generously to United Way. While not everybody likes it, some feel that the end justifies the means—it results in more money going to the needy.

Supporting United Way has become a way of life in corporate America. A company's 100 percent participation is viewed by many as a team effort. In many communities, companies with the highest percentage of employee contributions make the local news. For this reason, if you don't contribute, you risk being seen as a poor team player.

Furthermore, the amount of your contribution may be viewed by your coworkers and boss as a reflection of your character. After all, coworkers have an approximate idea of how much you make, and your boss knows exactly what your paycheck is.

May I add that I personally review contributions made by virtually all employees at MRI headquarters. And I form impressions of our people based on these reviews. Surely other bosses are likewise influenced. Thus a small contribution may reflect poorly on your concern for others. Likewise, a generous contribution demonstrates your true nature. Just the same, giving should come from the heart. If you plan to give but are not sure how much to contribute, give enough so it hurts a little. That's real charity.

SEE ALSO #76, #96, #128, #137, AND #157.

89. If You Share a Secretary, Don't Monopolize Her Time

MANY OF TODAY'S companies assign one secretary or administrative assistant to two or more people. If you share a secretary, you must be considerate of other people's needs to avoid conflict. In other words, don't monopolize the secretary's time! The last thing your boss needs is to have you and your coworkers bickering.

Sharing a secretary requires teamwork. To prevent friction, you must recognize other people's requirements so the secretary's time is allotted fairly. This requires a mutual respect for each other's work. And in the event of a crisis, one must give in to the needs of the other. Only by exhibiting mutual consideration can there be harmony.

A word of caution: never give a shared secretary personal errands. Delegate only business-related assignments to her. And when the secretary has a heavy workload, do things on your own—such as getting your own coffee and making your own copies.

90. Improve Your Listening Skills

MOST FOLKS THINK A great communicator is a person with excellent speaking skills. This is true to some extent, but speaking is only one part of effective communication. Listening is equally important. In fact, some people think being a good listener is the more valuable of the two skills, reasoning that because God gave us two ears and only one mouth, we are meant to do twice as much listening as speaking.

Obviously, you'll learn more from what other people say than from what you say. With this in mind, it is imperative to be a good listener. Listening well is a sign that you respect your superiors, especially your boss, and that you have good manners. And contrary to what some people think, you'll be a more interesting person if you listen intently when others are talking rather than trying to dominate the conversation by refusing to let anyone else voice an opinion.

Some people have a habit of interrupting before other people finish talking. It's a good idea for everyone to practice waiting briefly, say, half a second, before speaking. At MRI, we've learned the value of this pause quite unintentionally.

Our video conferencing network is the world's largest; we use it daily for class lectures and interviews. But its $1/6$-second sound delay makes it impossible to interrupt! We get great feedback from people praising this sound delay feature because it makes them pause, reflect, and allow the other person to finish his statement.

SEE ALSO #118.

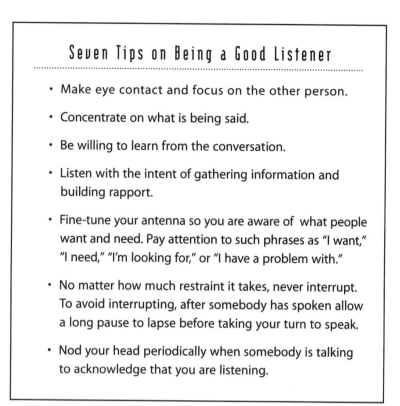

Seven Tips on Being a Good Listener

- Make eye contact and focus on the other person.

- Concentrate on what is being said.

- Be willing to learn from the conversation.

- Listen with the intent of gathering information and building rapport.

- Fine-tune your antenna so you are aware of what people want and need. Pay attention to such phrases as "I want," "I need," "I'm looking for," or "I have a problem with."

- No matter how much restraint it takes, never interrupt. To avoid interrupting, after somebody has spoken allow a long pause to lapse before taking your turn to speak.

- Nod your head periodically when somebody is talking to acknowledge that you are listening.

91. Don't Spill Your Guts to the Company Therapist

OFTEN, A COMPANY hires a psychiatrist to assess its employees. It's his job to evaluate your productivity, management skills, and emotional stability when you're a candidate for new job responsibilities. Knowing this, be stingy with personal information that you wouldn't want your boss and your boss's boss to know.

Say, for instance, senior management is considering you for a top position. In this scenario, keep in mind that you're being judged on how you are likely to react in a stressful situation, or how you handle pressure, and so on. In job evaluations of this nature, it's the counselor's job to report his findings up the corporate ladder. If you have a problem that could affect your productivity or your management skills, the company is paying him to find it.

If you're in need of therapy, this is not the time or place to discuss your personal hang-ups. Hire your own therapist to work out these problems. In general, a patient-therapist relationship is held under the strictest confidence. But when the psychiatrist is on the company payroll to size you up, that's a different ballgame.

92. Manage Your Time Effectively

ONE THING IS for sure—you'll never disappoint your boss by excelling at managing your time. After all, when you're on her payroll, you're working on her time. So the better you manage it, the more she will value you as an employee. Here are some tips for better time management:

- Allow some time for the unexpected.

- Focus on one thing at a time. When interrupted, take time to reach a comfortable stopping place.

- Set and communicate clear deadlines. Specify "Tuesday by 10 A.M." instead of "in a day or so."

- Set appointments at precise times (for example, 10:26 rather than 10:30). This will not only get people's attention, they'll be more punctual. At MRI, we often set candidate interviews this way. You will be amazed at how this technique prompts everyone to be on time.

- Handle each piece of mail only once: read it, then route, file, or trash it. Most people shuffle paper because they never complete this cycle.

- Keep a timer by your telephone and limit your conversations.

- Keep a written to-do list, and add to it all day long. At day's end, or early the next morning, prioritize the list. Don't depend on memory, especially overnight.

- Make the most of your time: it's the only thing everyone has the same amount of.

93. When You Have a Great Idea, Tell Your Boss Before Anyone Else

Your boss is the first person to whom you should present your big ideas. Never go over his head and share your idea with her boss or with someone even higher up the corporate ladder. If it's a winner, she'll report it to her boss, and she may or may not give the credit to you. While it is preferable for you to be commended for your idea, if you're not credited, let it go! What matters is that your boss knows it was your idea. By making a fuss over receiving credit, you'll lose the points you already scored with your boss.

94. Increase Your Walking Pace

By WALKING at a fast pace, you project an image that you are a busy, important person with a purpose. Conversely, people who shuffle along at a slow pace give the impression that they lack direction, have time to spare, and are lazy.

The pace at which you walk makes a difference in how people view you. For those of you who have been in military service, think back to how the appearance of being busy was a determining factor in avoiding getting picked to "volunteer" for a detail (a chore that nobody wanted). While the workplace is not the same as the military, the analogy is valid. People who mosey along at a slow pace give the impression that they are slackers. This is not an impression you want your boss to have about you. Try walking at a 25 percent faster pace than you normally walk. Not only will you get where you're going in 75 percent of the time, you'll also advance careerwise at a faster pace.

95. Learn the Names of Customers, Coworkers, Members of the Boss's Family, and the Boss's Friends

WANT TO MAKE a good impression on people who are important to your boss? One quick, sure way to do this is to learn the names of the boss's customers, family members, and personal friends. Why does this make such a good impression? It makes a person feel important when somebody has made the effort to learn her name. And when you make people feel important, they're more apt to like you. Never forget that the sweetest sounding word in any language is a person's name. When you think about it, remembering somebody's name is such a simple, thoughtful gesture, you'd think everyone would automatically do it. The fact is that most people are too lazy to make the effort. What a shame, because it's really so easy to do. One technique, for example: after an introduction, as soon as you realize that you've lost track of someone's name, ask him to repeat it to you again. He'll be flattered that you made the effort to tune in to him.

Because customers, family members, and friends are important people to your boss, be assured that a good word from one of them on your behalf is guaranteed to score big points. And any boss should apply the same to his ultimate boss—the customer. I try to know the names of each of my customers—the 700-plus MRI managers throughout the world.

96. Strive to Understand How the Whole Company Works

DON'T ALLOW YOURSELF to develop a case of tunnel vision, an insidious disease that limits people's thinking to only those areas within their own departments. When this infirmity sets in, it places severe restrictions on one's ability to advance up the corporate ladder.

This is true for three reasons. First, by having a narrow focus on a single part of the big picture, you lock yourself into a small area of the company, permanently restricting your growth to a single unit. This results in passing up opportunities for advancement in other areas. Furthermore, if the department were to close, your career would be severely jeopardized.

Second, by knowing about other areas, you are better able to relate to how your job ties in to other people's jobs throughout the entire company. In turn, with this understanding, you have a panoramic view of how your job ties in with the big picture. Since your boss probably sees the big picture, he'll delight in having you share it with him.

And third, you will be capable of cross-pollinating ideas— taking an idea from one department and applying it to still another department.

SEE ALSO #18, #76, #88, #128, #137, AND #157.

97. Get into the Habit of Speaking Up

EMPLOYEES WHO HAVE little or nothing to say generally aren't highly regarded by management. Withholding your opinions and ideas is as useless as not having them. Remember, you're being paid to think, so until you communicate your thoughts, your company isn't getting its money's worth.

Unfortunately, many people tend to remain silent due to their fear of addressing an audience or creating conflict with superiors. Hence, they keep their thoughts to themselves during meetings. Some people clam up even during one-on-one conferences with their bosses.

If you have something important to say in your area of expertise, failure to express that thought amounts to withholding pertinent information from your company. Depending on its relevance, it could even be a reason for your dismissal. This is true because your compensation is based, in part, on your knowledge, which is an accumulation of your background, training, and experience. In other words, you are obligated to speak out—it's your responsibility.

Four Tips on Speaking Up

- Mentally rehearse what you want to say. It's OK to refer to notes if you need them—they are a good indication that you came prepared.

- Stick to your main point. Even if someone gets emotional and inadvertently (or purposely) sidetracks you, don't respond. Instead get back to your point.

- Don't be close-minded. Listen to points made by others, and if someone else's point is relevant, integrate it in with yours.

- Help others speak up. At a meeting, be sure everyone is given time to express an opinion, even if you must single out that person to ask them to express an opinion.

98. Always Express Gratitude When Your Boss Does Something on Your Behalf

WHEN YOUR BOSS does a favor for you—no matter how small— be sure to make your appreciation known. Even though her motive wasn't to be thanked, she still deserves your thanks for two reasons: first, because it's common courtesy, and second, your boss is like the rest of us—we all want to be appreciated for our acts of generosity.

As a sign of goodwill, smart employees look for reasons to express gratitude to their bosses. Thanking a boss for anything major such as a salary increase or a promotion is obvious: it would be impolite to say nothing. Likewise, don't overlook the little things your boss does for you such as asking your opinion on a new product, inviting you to sit in during a meeting to discuss a high-level business plan, and so on.

When you shower your boss with gratitude, her response will be to do still more on your behalf. This response is just basic human nature, so take advantage of it!

99. Express Congratulations or Sympathy When Appropriate

HERE'S AN INSTANCE where a miniscule effort on your part can mean a big boost for someone's feelings. Congratulating people on their achievements should be done automatically, without the slightest hesitation. You'll read about this people skill in practically any relationship book you pick up. That's because it's so effective—and easy to do.

These same books say that by giving to others, you'll get back in spades. In the world of business, when you express your sincere congratulations on another's success, you are viewed as a team player. It also makes you appear to be an individual with good self-esteem—someone who has enough belief in his own self-worth that he isn't threatened by someone else's success.

You are seen in the same favorable light when you express your sympathy to someone who is experiencing sorrow or disappointment. When a coworker or associate suffers a setback, a few kind words are always appreciated. Offer a sincere comment such as, "I admire your effort, and I know you'll succeed the next time around," or, "I want you to know I'm rooting for you, and I know good people like you eventually win." It takes so little effort to say a few words of encouragement, and when they are said at the right time, these kind words are not only greatly appreciated but long remembered.

Don't be shy about communicating these sentiments to your boss when she suffers a setback. Just because she's the boss, don't assume she doesn't need a few words of encouragement like everyone else.

100. Read the Publications Your Boss Reads

IF A PUBLICATION is important enough for your boss to read, you should be reading it, too. Every industry has its own publications, and you can be sure that the top people in the field read them cover to cover. Professionals want to know everything that's going on in the industry. They want to read about trends, new ideas, and most importantly, who's doing what. In this area, they read any information they can regarding their competitors.

Depending on your position, your boss may *expect* you to read the industry publications. If this is so, and you don't, his opinion of your professionalism will slip a notch or two. When you are having lunch with your boss, mentioning an article in the most recent publication serves as an excellent icebreaker.

101. Return Phone Calls Promptly

ONE THING YOU can bet on: you won't win friends or influence people by failing to return their phone calls. Failing to return calls is rude and offensive. It clearly sends a message to the caller that you don't think she's important enough to warrant your reply. Do it to the wrong person, or do it enough times, and you risk having people say unkind words about you to your boss.

If you're simply so busy that you can't possibly squeeze returning calls into your day, do it after working hours. If that makes it impossible to contact people, ask your secretary to make the calls for you with your sincerest apologies. Be sure to instruct him to set up a convenient time when you can return each call.

102. Be on Time

LOOKING FOR ANOTHER way to insult people? Show them how little you respect their time by being late for an appointment or meeting—or even better, just put them on hold when they call you, and leave them hanging there while you talk to someone else. When you keep people waiting, your action is saying to them, "My time is valuable and yours isn't. So you can just twiddle your thumbs while you wait for me."

That's not the kind of message you want to send to people in the business world. (It's not a good way to treat your family and friends either.) Your boss may pick up still another message that will be detrimental to your career. Tardy people who can't manage their time give the impression they are disorganized and out of control. Bear in mind, irresponsible people aren't heavy favorites to be promoted.

103. Be Sensitive to Others' Problems

EVEN THOUGH THEY shouldn't, some people can't help bringing their personal problems with them to the office. This practice is bound to affect their work. Although many management books tell you not to get involved in other people's personal lives, such indifference is not a solution. When a subordinate, a coworker, or even your boss is distracted by what's happening at home, it is an interruption in the workplace. Ignoring the problem isn't going to make it go away.

Let's say you work side by side with a coworker who is troubled with a personal problem—for example, a sick spouse, a nasty divorce, or pressure from creditors. This individual isn't an office fixture, she's a warm body with emotions. When she's upset, ignoring her anxieties is insensitive and unsympathetic. While it's not wise to dwell on problems during office hours, you must show some personal concern. Perhaps just letting her know you care will suffice, or offer your support during lunch or for a few minutes after work.

No matter what the textbooks tell you about not becoming emotionally involved in people's personal lives, how can you remain aloof when you work side by side with someone eight hours a day? Only cold, callous people can avoid displaying personal feelings under these circumstances. Such people make poor team players, for not only do they lack communication skills, they inspire no loyalty among their subordinates. Don't put yourself in this category—you can do better.

104. Provide Criticism Privately

JUST AS YOU should praise in public, you should criticize in private. While some managers like to make an example of a subordinate by reading the riot act to him in the presence of others, this form of mental abuse is damaging to morale. Public criticism humiliates the individual at the receiving end and upsets everyone within earshot. It puts people on notice that they, too, can be the target of similar degradation.

It's far more effective to gently offer constructive criticism in a private conversation, *always* behind closed doors. This protects morale and increases the chances that your criticism will be well-received. If you calmly discuss your dissatisfaction, listening to the other person's explanation, nobody walks away with a feeling of devastation.

SEE ALSO #20, #28, AND #45.

105. Be Modest

IN A WELL-MANAGED company, the cream eventually rises to the top. If you're as good as you think you are, everyone will soon find out without your having to promote yourself by bragging.

You'll stand out far more for your modesty than your lack of humility. Nobody likes a braggart—so when you get the urge to toot your own horn, resist the temptation. It will only make you look bad in the eyes of others.

Actually, trying to promote yourself does the opposite of what it is intended to do—it is self-defeating. While your intent may be to draw their attention to your proficiency, you are more likely to be viewed as an insecure individual who needs to draw attention to herself.

In business, braggarts are viewed as poor team players unwilling to share the glory of the team's success but instead wanting to hog it for themselves. So avoid bragging at all costs. It is never appropriate, and no matter how subtle you think you are, you're not apt to fool anyone. When you brag, people will recognize it for what it is. Let your actions, your accomplishments, and your vitality at work do your bragging for you.

106. Allow Others to Save Face

SOME PEOPLE DELIGHT in the misery of others. Making another person look inferior makes them feel superior. While this behavior may be a source of instant gratification, it creates no long-term goodwill. Instead, it generates resentment and bitterness.

When somebody makes a mistake, he's usually the first to know about it, so you don't have to rub his nose in it. It's better to turn your head the other way and spare him embarrassment.

Allowing someone to save face is an act of kindness. You can help someone avoid the distress and discomfort that accompanies a mistake. People know when you know they were wrong, and they appreciate your benevolence when you overlook it.

107. Keep Business in the Office

MANY COMPANIES ARE so security-conscious about the information that flows around the office, visitors must wear identification badges while on the premises. Company business is company business, and all employees should respect its confidentiality.

Be especially careful about discussing company affairs with coworkers in a public area. Too often, employees discuss confidential information in a restaurant without having any idea who may be sitting at the next table or the booth behind them. You just never know when an unfriendly eavesdropper may be listening in on the conversation. Knowing this, it's mind-boggling how much inappropriate conversation that should be reserved for discussion behind closed doors goes on in public places.

The same applies to discussing classified company business at your own dining room table with your family. Your spouse or children might pick something up and inadvertently repeat it to the wrong person.

Likewise, don't try to impress outsiders with how important you are to your company by divulging inside information to them. If the wrong information leaks and it's traced to your big mouth, you'll be in big trouble.

108. Keep Small Talk to a Minimum

THERE ARE MANY ways people waste their precious time, but at the top of the list is small talk. Unlike other time killers, small talk wastes not just one person's time, but that of two people or even more.

Some people mistake small talk for networking. When you engage in idle chatter about subjects such as sports, the weather, or a current political campaign, it has nothing to do with networking. When such conversations are conducted in the office, you're wasting your time, and that of the person with whom you're conversing.

And note that, while E-mail and the Internet are great workplace tools, they are also opportunities to take small talk to a technological extreme. Avoid useless E-mail and time-wasting Internet surfing on company time.

Six Ways to Avoid Small Talk

- Tell coworkers who want to chat that you have a deadline to meet, an appointment to keep, or a meeting to prepare for.

- Keep a timer by your phone so your conversations are limited to five minutes or less.

- Plan every meeting with a specific cutoff time.

- Limit your conversations to business-related subjects only.

- When you enter somebody's office for a brief visit, never sit down.

- Avoid personal calls or E-mail during office hours.

109. Never Burn Bridges

SUCCESSFUL BUSINESSPEOPLE build their success by establishing long-term relationships with many people. These relationships are accumulated over many years with hundreds of people inside and outside their company. Their networking covers a wide array of contacts they've accumulated within and even outside of their industry.

You never know whether someone you come into contact with may influence your career in the future. A new trainee may be tagged for the company's fast track and within a short period enjoy an accelerated climb to the top of the corporate ladder. A secretary may be hired as your boss's or CEO's secretary, and in this capacity become an invaluable ally. On your climb up the corporate ladder, treat all people you pass with courtesy and respect—you may meet them again on your way back down!

Above all, don't write off anyone who served as your ally in the past but is no longer in a position to benefit you. A "What have you done for me lately?" attitude turns former friends into foes. Be grateful to such friends and pledge your lifelong loyalty to them. Such loyalty is an admirable quality, and if you regularly display it, your boss is bound to take notice. When she observes your loyalty to others, she'll rightfully assume that you're a loyal person, and that she too will be the recipient of your loyalty.

Keep in contact with people by sending them greeting cards and calling them occasionally. Also, get in the habit of sending them magazine and newspaper articles about their special interests they might have missed. And when you come across an article about them, tear it out and send it with a personal note congratulating them.

110. Be Sensitive to Office Politics

EVEN THOUGH YOU may not consider yourself political, you should be in tune with your company's office politics. Although unwritten, a company's politics may play as important a role as its formal written code. There may be a 200-page looseleaf notebook spelling out company policy that was put together in the mid-1980s by a management consulting firm that has long since been let go. While a hefty fee was paid to put it together, nobody paid any attention to it back then, and for sure, nobody does today. Just because it's in writing doesn't mean it's the official position of management. More importantly, on matters like bonuses, promotions, and severance pay, you should be aware of current precedent.

When it comes to politics, you also have to know the players. In this regard, sometimes a person's title can be misleading. A senior executive could have an impressive title but no influence in upper-management circles. Likewise, the young kid in the mailroom may turn out to be the CEO's nephew.

In some companies the title of vice president is far more important than it is where you work. In some organizations, nothing gets accomplished in committees, while in others, everything does. The list goes on and on.

III. Do Not Drink

If you're going to drink at lunch, it's always better to drink whiskey than vodka. That's because it's better for people to think you're drunk than to think you're stupid! Of course, either way, you can't win. So the best advice is not to drink any alcohol during your workday. I've never yet met a boss who encouraged employees to drink!

Even if you work alone, stay away from alcohol. There is no upside, but there is a downside. Aside from the fact that you could end up with a drinking problem, there's nothing to be gained from a drink or two. Even a single drink can make you sleepy. And contrary to what some people think, alcohol doesn't enhance your creativity—it dulls your senses. If you think you need booze to be creative, you may have a problem.

While it's tempting to take a drink "just to be social" when others are having one at lunch, learn to say no. As one Fortune 500 company CEO reports, "I always tell people, 'One drink makes me sleepy and two make me high, so I pass.'" Of course, he's being diplomatic, but even that's not necessary. It's sufficient to simply say no.

112. Learn to Compromise

LIFE IS FULL of compromises. This is particularly applicable in the workplace, because business is a matter of give and take. It's not reasonable to always expect to get your way, unless, of course, you're the boss. And even then, good bosses are never so demanding—or so unreasonable.

Since this is a book about scoring points with your boss, it's safe to assume you're not in a position to be so inflexible that you never compromise. You must be willing to compromise in most areas, with the exception, that is, of principles.

Remember too, there's usually more than one way to skin a cat. Even though you may think you have a perfect solution to a problem or an ideal way to implement a project, there may be still other ways. Don't be so bullheaded as to think that your way is the only way. Sometimes, too, even though your way may be best, if your boss and coworkers don't buy into it, it probably won't fly. A mediocre idea that has everyone's support is better than a superior idea that no one supports. It's good to keep this in mind with decisions that require compromise.

SEE ALSO #75.

113. Don't Try to Be Popular

THE OBJECT OF business is not to win a popularity contest, so you don't have to be "Mr. Nice Guy" all the time. While it's noble to try to be benevolent to everyone with whom you come in contact, business situations may at times require you to do something unpopular like discipline or even discharge a subordinate. Or you might have to express disapproval of someone who is up for promotion, turn down a proposal, or say no to someone's brilliant idea—the list goes on and on. While you may be sensitive, some actions you have to take will cause some people to think negatively of you from time to time. This is part of your job—you can't always be agreeable just because you don't want to hurt somebody's feelings.

As Harry Truman said, "If you can't stand the heat, get out of the kitchen." In business, you sometimes have to make a decision that isn't popular with everyone; in the process, some people will be upset. Always pleasing everybody is not possible, so don't even think about it. To paraphrase Abraham Lincoln, you can't please all of the people all of the time.

Of course, this means there will be occasions when you must even say no to your boss. For instance, he may ask you to work overtime on a night when you promised your daughter you'd attend her class play. Chances are, he will respect your commitment to your family.

114. Always Use Appropriate, Professional Language

It goes without saying that cursing and politically incorrect language don't belong in the workplace. It doesn't matter if you work at an office where your colleagues fail to curb their language. Using appropriate, professional language doesn't automatically make you a prude. You can be one of the gang and still maintain your professionalism. Women in particular, in an attempt to penetrate the glass ceiling, may adopt stereotyped male behavior and as a result diminish their personal charm. Women need not compromise their femininity to be effective in today's workplace.

Even if your boss uses four-letter words, he won't be impressed if you do. After all, wrong is wrong. So don't think you're scoring points with him by emulating his bad habits, because you aren't!

On the subject of professional language, note that certain buzzwords and acronyms that are OK to use with your peers are inappropriate among outsiders. Using shoptalk that is unfamiliar to others is simply a poor way to communicate. Not only does it make people feel uncomfortable around you, they'll probably wonder what the heck you're talking about.

115. Show Loyalty by Keeping Confidences

To PUT IT BLUNTLY, don't be a blabbermouth! When you're told something in confidence, you have an obligation to keep it to yourself; otherwise, you violate the trust another person has in you. This is a moral obligation in and out of the workplace.

In the workplace, however, it goes even further. Divulging information can be very costly if that information falls into the wrong hands. Telling a customer, another employee, or worse, a competitor, about something you've been privy to, can severely damage your company. And in the case of a publicly owned corporation, disclosing inside information is a violation of securities law—you can go to prison for it!

Now, you can imagine what your boss would think if you betrayed her by discussing with others what she confided to you. You'll be getting off easy if she merely thinks you're a gossip, but she could easily accuse you of disloyalty. In either scenario, once your boss feels you can't be trusted with confidences, she'll make certain you are never again privy to sensitive information.

116. With a New Boss, Find Your Parameters

BOSSES ARE DIFFERENT; no two are alike. So early in the game, it's important to ascertain your boundaries with your new boss.

Knowing the ground rules will ease the transition for both of you. Knowing exactly what is required of you in terms of your relationship with your boss beyond your job description is essential. For instance, which decisions are you able to make on your own, and which decisions require your boss's involvement? How aggressively can you pursue certain matters on your own initiative without his approval?

When you engage in dialogue with your new boss, have a list of questions to present. Your preparedness will make a good first impression. But try to keep the discussion informal. Remember, at this stage you're just beginning to feel each other out.

117. Be Open to New Ideas

IT'S COMMON FOR people to resist change because it's easier to continue doing things the current way. Doing something new means taking a risk that things might not be as good as they are now. However, in today's fast-changing world, it's essential to be open to new ideas. Individuals and companies that feel too comfortable are stuck in complacency, a state of being that spells disaster. If your boss senses that you are closed to new ideas, it could be detrimental to your chances of promotion. Remember, change is essential, and people who resist change are viewed as dinosaurs.

In the same way, don't be so rigid about your ideas that you refuse to accept somebody else's. Be open-minded and willing to hear others out. Who knows? No matter how good your idea may be, somebody may have an even better one. Then too, perhaps the combination of yours and theirs will result in an idea superior to both. As Oliver Wendell Holmes said, "Many times ideas grow better when transplanted from one mind to another."

118. Develop Your People Skills

IN OUR COMPUTER-DEPENDENT world, it's easy to get so caught up in developing our technical skills that we neglect our people skills. After all, what we read in our old science fiction books about machines someday replacing human beings has already been happening for years. So there's good reason for us to be concerned, realizing that if our technical skills are not on the cutting edge, our worth in the workplace will dwindle.

All of the above is true: you should have a lifetime self-improvement program in place to continually enhance your technical skills. Just don't do it at the expense of your people skills.

It's probable that in the competition for middle- and senior-management positions there will be a shortage of candidates with people skills. That's too bad, because when you get right down to it, every business is a people business. As our society becomes more complex, no machine can ever replace employees with strong people skills. As people are forced to deal more and more with the cold mediums of self-service, E-mail, voice mail, and ATM machines, which represent the epitome of impersonalization in corporate America, the demand for individuals with people skills will continue to grow.

So while you're investing in self-improvement courses or reading the latest how-to book, don't forget to recognize the need for employees with people skills, and brush up on yours.

SEE ALSO #90.

119. Take the Initiative in Solving an Irate Customer's Problem

THE BOTTOM LINE of every company is how well it takes care of its customers—they are the reason the business exists in the first place. That's why most successful companies are willing to bend over backward for their customers.

However, no matter how hard a company strives to serve its customers, it's not possible to please all of them all the time. That's why every so often even the best company is going to have a dissatisfied customer.

Knowing this, whenever you have the opportunity, always be willing to make an extra effort to soothe an irate customer. Even if it's "not your job," go out of your way to smooth things out, because no customers means no company—it's as simple as that! Do it because it *is* part of your job, whether you normally have direct contact with customers or not. The fact is, it's everyone's job!

One more thing: don't go running to your boss for a pat on the head after every close encounter with a customer. In time, word about your finesse with customers will spread throughout the company. In fact, you'll find that those customers who were the most irritated and difficult will become your most ardent supporters. They will let your superiors know what you did for them. As you'll discover, it's better for your boss to hear about you from customers raving with delight than from you.

120. Help Your Boss Stay on Schedule

LET'S ASSUME THAT your boss's time is more valuable than yours. (Even if it isn't, she thinks it is.) With this in mind, you too must place a high value on her time. One way you can play a supportive role in this capacity is to help keep her on schedule.

Of course, this is easier said than done. This demanding task will sometimes require you to schedule your work around her time needs. This may require some overtime on your part to catch up with your work. Nonetheless, when your boss has an important task to perform and is running behind schedule, you should step in to assist her. Employees who give their bosses a hand at such crucial times are truly appreciated.

121. Don't Rush Through a Job in an Effort to Impress Your Boss

To MAKE A GOOD impression on the boss, many people go into fast-forward mode to complete the task at hand. Perhaps they do so because the boss places a high value on time. Sure, efficiency is great—but as the saying goes, haste makes waste. If your rush to impress your boss results in sloppy work, what kind of impression does that make? Your boss may have a different interpretation. He could regard your hasty performance as a sign of contempt for your work.

When an assignment is over, few will remember how long it took to complete, but no one will forget the quality of your work. So never sacrifice quality in the name of expediency. In your rush to finish a job, don't cut back on the planning, research, or proofreading needed to display your best work. It's far more important for your boss to be impressed with the quality of your work rather than how quickly it is completed.

122. Remember Special Occasions

A RECENT SURVEY revealed that the average American adult receives only six birthday cards a year. So you can be sure that the card you send your boss will certainly be appreciated. One thing is certain—it won't get lost in the shuffle.

It's a good idea to keep a calendar or a datebook marked with your boss's birthday, wedding anniversary, and other special occasions. Mark the date to send the card on your calendar a few days in advance, because a late card loses some of its effectiveness. A card or personal letter congratulating your boss on an award or honor he received is always appropriate. And while you're at it, get in the habit of sending thank-you notes and get-well cards, too. An inexpensive gift like flowers or lunch is always appreciated.

Because it's such a good idea to remember your boss's special occasions, you ought to do the same with your coworkers. Considering the amount of goodwill this gesture creates, it takes very little effort. If you have a reputation among the people you work with as a thoughtful person, you are projecting the positive image you want around the office.

123. Tell Your Boss What a Great Day You're Having

HAVING A GREAT DAY? If so, don't keep it a secret—don't be shy about announcing it to your boss and coworkers. Tell people about how much you're enjoying such a wonderful day, and it's certain that your warmth will become contagious. At the very least, people will make a conscious effort not to rain on your parade.

Highly successful people have great days practically every day. Their positive attitude is a significant contributing factor to their success. It's a fact that positive things happen to people with positive attitudes. Good days spawn more good days.

124. Maintain a Positive Attitude

UNDOUBTEDLY, IT'S futile to tell you about the importance of having an upbeat, positive attitude in a single entry of this book. After all, volumes have been written on the subject, and even those people who read entire books on maintaining a positive mental attitude find that it takes more than a book to make a dent in a negative attitude. However, not mentioning it in this book would be negligent because a positive attitude is vital to both scoring points with your boss and attaining success in all your endeavors.

Your boss will be best served if you maintain an upbeat, positive attitude. No one wants to work with a person who is negative. A successful, thriving business is just that because its workplace is upbeat and its people look toward the future with optimism. It's a place where people set goals they intend to reach, and their objective is to generate a profit—not a loss. Successful bosses surround themselves with upbeat, positive people.

Five Reasons to Think Positively

- It will give you a surge of adrenaline that will provide you with additional energy.
- Your work will be more enjoyable.
- You will provide inspiration to others, and, in turn, people will rally around you.
- It will give you direction and help you get where you want to go.
- It's good for your general health.

125. Never Make an Idle Threat to Your Boss

....

DON'T THREATEN YOUR boss that you'll quit if you don't get a pay raise, a promotion, or if such-and-such doesn't happen. Nobody likes to be threatened, and idle threats are annoying.

How would you like it if your boss regularly threatened to fire you when she wasn't satisfied with your work? Not only would this treatment provoke you, it would leave you with a feeling of insecurity. Likewise, threatening to quit is analogous to your boss threatening to fire you. If she values your work, the possibility of losing you will upset her. However, in time, the continuance of idle threats will so exasperate her that she'll begin to look around for somebody to replace you. Once she gets in this mind-set, you're a goner.

126. Be Reserved at Company Parties

DON'T GO CRAZY at company shindigs. Although you may be away from the office, remember that you're there on company business. Too often, people let their hair down at these affairs, only to regret it the following Monday morning at the office.

At the top of the list of what's considered poor behavior is excessive drinking. When the food and drinks are on the house, people tend to overindulge. Don't consume more alcohol than you can handle!

Frequently, people tend to get too chummy with the boss, secretary, or coworkers when in a cozy environment away from the workplace. Especially after a drink or two, it's natural to relax and let your hair down. Of course, this is the idea—you're supposed to enjoy yourself at such functions. Just don't overdo it by doing something you'll regret later. Things not to do range from wearing the proverbial lamp shade on your head to putting the make on that cute secretary who you *think* has a crush on you.

Since you're there to have a good time, avoid limiting conversation to talking shop, and, as usual, stay away from discussing controversial topics with your coworkers. While there are certainly no-nos, there are still a lot of things you can do to have a wonderful time. So enjoy!

127. Stay Focused

ANYONE WHO HAS ever played sports understands what a difference focus makes. In golf, for instance, getting or losing concentration can make an immediate difference of several strokes to your game. In a highly contested sports event, intensity of this nature is an essential competitive edge.

In the world of business, you can assure peak performance by staying focused on a specific assignment. In the workplace, you may have several assignments that require your attention during the course of a given period. When this is so, your highest-priority assignment must receive your undivided attention. During the heat of the day, when there's a lot of pressure to complete all of your work, it may be difficult to concentrate on one assignment at a time. For this reason, unorganized people are often unable to get their priorities straight. Consequently, they work helter-skelter, trying to do a little of everything at the same time and accomplishing very little. This is not a good way to score points with your boss.

Your success hinges on your ability to focus on one step at a time. A tall skyscraper is built one brick at a time, a magnificent oil painting is painted one brush stroke at a time, and a book is written one word at a time. So while it's essential to keep your eye on the big picture, never lose focus on the small, seemingly insignificant details required to achieve your long-term goal. Do outstandingly well at what you do today, this week, and this month. Tomorrow will take care of itself by the brilliant job you do today.

128. Be a Good Corporate Citizen

SUCCESSFUL BUSINESSPEOPLE have an obligation to pay their dues by giving something back to the community. In large corporations, middle and senior managers are expected to become involved in the community, giving generously with both their time and money. As a result, in a majority of the leading companies, a high percentage of the executives put in many hours in community involvement. Check out the ways your company's top executives serve the community, and consider that an example for you to follow.

Certainly, community involvement makes demands on your time and energy, two things you may feel you don't have enough of. I've often wondered what other managers do from 5 to 10 P.M. This is the time I'm able to devote to good causes in the community, trying to make a difference in other people's lives. It still allows me time for dinner, although occasionally it may mean skipping a meal. Many of my weekends are also spent giving to the community. Over the years, I estimate I've averaged at least 20 hours a week. While I may have made some personal sacrifices, that's the price of fulfilling an obligation. And that's exactly what it is—an obligation.

Like any other CEO, I'm concerned when I observe key managers who are not putting in as much office time as I'd prefer. However, if I see them giving time to the community, I feel more comfortable. It's difficult to quantify how the company directly benefits from its people's community involvement, but we do know it's bound to have a positive influence on our corporate image. And, in the long run, our reputation is one of our most valuable assets.

Rather than being active in many community activities and not having enough time to make a significant difference in any, carefully select one worthy cause to which you can make a major commitment. With so many good charitable and civic causes in need of your participation, you will have plenty of options, so choose one you can serve with a passion.

While your sole purpose should be to serve the community, these extracurricular activities are an excellent source for making contacts with business leaders. As an extra bonus to the built-in networking, you'll enjoy the good feeling of knowing you're helping others. Senior management is certain to consider your community involvement an important factor when you're reviewed for future promotions. It's a fact that many of today's leading companies list good citizenship in the community as one of its core corporate values.

SEE ALSO #18, #76, #88, #96, #137, AND #157.

129. Plan Time Off When It's Good for Your Boss, and Let Her Know in Advance

ASSUMING THAT YOUR boss depends on you, be sure to coordinate your time off by giving her enough advance notice. This means letting her know at least six weeks before you take off for vacation. Even certain kinds of surgery can be scheduled weeks ahead of the operation date. Of course, if there's a baby due in the family, the delivery date is fairly predictable.

With some bosses, it's desirable for you to plan your vacations to coincide exactly with hers. In other instances, this will be the worst time for you to be off because it's essential for one of you to be there when the other is not available.

Depending upon how indispensable you are, your boss may never find it totally convenient for you to take time off. While you want her to think she can't do without you, you do need your vacation time, which she realizes as well.

130. Train Someone to Replace You in Case You Get Promoted

SOME PEOPLE THINK that by making themselves irreplaceable, they're guaranteed lifetime job security. In some situations they may be right, but if they have ambitions to advance up the corporate ladder, they're being shortsighted.

What often happens is a dilemma: the boss can't promote such an employee because no one else can fill his slot! To avoid this situation, make sure you've trained somebody to step into your present position so when it's time for you to be promoted, you can pass the baton to someone behind you. If you fail to do this, you might lose an opportunity to advance.

Failing to train somebody to replace you sends a negative message to management. First, it indicates you're not a team player. Second, it announces to the world that you feel threatened—that you feel having a trained backup person would endanger your job security. Even if it would, that's a gamble you have to take.

131. Don't Try to Be the Office Peacock

WHILE YOU SHOULD always be concerned about your appearance, there's such a thing as overkill. The office is not a place to strut like a peacock, flaunting an expensive wardrobe. Not only is this behavior in poor taste, it distracts others from their work. You don't want a reputation as the person in the office who causes everyone to whisper, or worse, whistle, when you enter the room. Nor do you want them to roll their eyes each time they see you walk in wearing a new outfit. Although in many areas you want to stand above the crowd, this is not one of them. It's not a wise way to get the attention of your boss.

Overdressing can also have a negative effect on morale. You may cause some of your coworkers to feel they have to keep up with you; competition of this nature is not desirable in the workplace. Not only does it result in unfriendly competition, it can be a source of resentment for those who can't afford to play the game. A single working mother with three children, for instance, is not likely to have the same clothing budget as a married working woman without young ones at home.

It's never in good taste to overdress—particularly in the workplace, where it's better to be understated than to flash a gaudy image. And on "casual day," the same rules apply. Certain casual attire is simply inappropriate in the workplace. There's such a thing as being too casual—wearing sandals or short shorts. However, some casual forms of dress may be acceptable, depending on the industry. For example, wearing sandals on casual day might be acceptable if you work for a company that manufactures beach attire, but not in a New York securities office.

132. Befriend Your Boss's Secretary

MAKE AN ALLY OF your boss's secretary. While some may not view her as an influential person in your organization, remember that she has a direct line to your boss's ear. In this capacity, she's in a position to do a lot of small favors for people she likes.

A personal secretary has the power to put your calls through, set up an appointment, give you the scoop on the mood the boss is in, and put in a good word about you to your boss. Don't underestimate the influence of her opinion. The tone in which she speaks about you can generate either positive or negative vibes. For example, she could tell her boss, "Bob Johnson is on the phone. Pick up line one." Or she can give the same message to her boss in a negative way: "Bob Johnson is on the line. Shall I tell him you're tied up?" Likewise, she can have a smile or a frown on her face when your name is mentioned—her facial expressions and body language send an important message to your boss. Although a secretary is not a high-ranking executive, she's in a position to influence your boss's reaction to you. Knowing this, make an effort to befriend her. Treat her with respect and warmth so you always have her in your corner.

133. Develop a Healthy Belief in the Impossible

As we approach the 21st century, we can look back on thousands of things that were said to be impossible at the beginning of this century. Who would have thought we would walk on the moon or receive messages from satellites in space? Everyday conveniences that we take for granted now were once considered science fiction—television, jet airplanes, copying machines, fax machines, and cellular telephones. We have lived in a computerized world for several decades. Yet the computer that in the 1950s occupied the space of a large room and cost $500,000 can now fit on your lap and typically costs about $2,000! We now know that what the mind can conceive, we can ultimately achieve.

The knowledge of what has been achieved during the past century should give each of us a healthy belief in the impossible. Don't back away from a challenge or assignment when the naysayers claim it can't be done. Just because something seemed impossible before doesn't mean you shouldn't attempt to tackle it head-on now. Don't allow roadblocks—real or imaginary—to discourage you from attempting the impossible.

Isn't it interesting that 50 years ago it was generally accepted that no one could run a mile in under four minutes? Although some runners came close, even scientists and physicians felt it wasn't possible for a human being to run at such a speed. Then came Great Britain's Roger Bannister, who ran the mile in 3 minutes and 59.4 seconds. Three months later, Roger Bannister and John Landy were pitted against each other in what was billed as "The Mile Race of the Century." Bannister's winning time was 3 minutes, 58.8 seconds and Landy clocked in at 3 minutes, 59.6 seconds. The four-minute barrier has since been broken rather routinely. But until Bannister did it, few dreamed it could be done. Today, the world record is 3 minutes, 46.32 seconds.

134. Update Your Spouse or Companion on Pertinent Business Information When Attending a Business Event

THE IMPRESSION MADE by the spouse or companion who accompanies you to a business event influences how you're viewed at work. After all, people are bound to judge you by the company you keep.

With this in mind, you want to make sure your companion comes across as intelligent and informed. This is not to imply that you should divulge inside information to this person—that's a definite no-no. However, your companion should have some general knowledge about your company, especially anything newsworthy that's happened lately.

Another reason to keep this person informed is so she will feel at ease with your business associates. We've all experienced that uncomfortable feeling of being the odd person out among a group of people, that awkwardness when you're the only one in a crowd who doesn't understand why everyone else is laughing.

A spouse, in particular, will feel uncomfortable because people assume he should have some basic knowledge of what you do for a living. When it becomes obvious to others that he doesn't, it gives the impression either that he's not smart or that he lacks interest in your career. It could be interpreted as meaning you don't communicate with your spouse. Take your pick—any one of the above is an unfavorable impression you don't want to make.

Remember too, when selecting between two employees for the same position, with all other factors being equal, some bosses may be prone to choose the candidate with the most impressive spouse. Depending on the job, a supportive spouse can be a tremendous asset—and bosses know it!

135. Know Your Worth

THROUGHOUT THIS BOOK, you have been advised to prepare before entering a meeting, calling on a customer, and so on. Entering into a discussion with your boss about increasing your wages also requires that you first do your homework. This applies to negotiating anything. If you enter into a negotiation half-cocked, you put yourself at a disadvantage. When approaching your boss for a raise, lack of preparation can cost you.

It's much like when you discuss the price of any product or service—you need some knowledge of the going rate. After all, your services are a commodity. It's no different than if you were seeking a house painter or a carpenter to bid on a job for your house. If it's a costly job, chances are you'd shop around to get an idea of the fair market value for the contractor's services. When you sit down to talk with your boss about a salary increase, you should know what you're worth in the job market. With this knowledge, you won't settle for too little, nor will you embarrass yourself by asking for an outlandish amount.

Also be sure to go into your discussion armed with reasons you deserve a raise. Prepare a presentation that elaborates on your accomplishments and the goals you plan to achieve in the future. Naturally, your objective is to sell your boss on why you're worth the extra money you're asking.

One important thing to keep in mind: When seeking a pay raise, never give a personal reason such as, "I'm having trouble meeting my monthly payments," "The alimony I'm paying is killing me," or "I have three kids in college." Your needs for a higher salary are not valid reasons to receive a pay raise. If you can't live within your means, that's your problem, not your boss's.

One final note: don't underestimate your worth. When in doubt about how much to ask, lean toward the high side. A good negotiator knows that once she sets her price, she can't ask for more but she can always come down!

136. Remember, Your Boss Is Lonely at the Top

To SOME PEOPLE, the expression "It's lonely at the top" is hard to imagine. After all, isn't the head honcho surrounded by underlings who are constantly reporting to him, always at his beck and call? How could anyone in that position be lonely?

It's not so much a matter of being alone as being out of touch with what's happening throughout the organization and in the field with customers. The feeling of loneliness comes more from feeling isolated than actually being alone. Up in his ivory tower, the boss often hears only what subordinates think he wants to hear. As a consequence, he's kept in the dark about things nobody wants him to know.

This opens a window of opportunity for you when you tell it to your boss like it really is. When he sees he can always rely on you to be straightforward, over time you'll enjoy a special rapport with your boss. This places you at a unique advantage shared only by his closest confidantes.

SEE ALSO #64.

137. If the Company Has Not Yet Developed a Mission Statement, Volunteer to Help Write One

ALTHOUGH EVERY COMPANY should have a mission statement, with the exception of the Fortune 500 companies, a majority do not. This is particularly true of small companies with less than 100 employees. If you work for a company that doesn't have a mission statement, volunteer to help write one. It's an excellent opportunity to score major points with your boss.

Here are a few suggestions on how to get started putting together a mission statement. Contact companies that already have one and ask for a copy of it. Generally, mission statements are public information—you might even find one listed in the annual report of a publicly owned company. Studying other mission statements will give you good ideas about how to create one for your company.

Interview people at all levels in your organization and ask them what they think belongs in your company's mission statement. By getting people to articulate their thoughts about your company's values, you'll soon have a clear idea what they are.

Remember, a mission statement doesn't have to be more than a page in length. Generally, the shorter the better—it should be brief enough to be printed on a wallet-sized laminated card.

SEE ALSO #76, #96, #128, AND #157.

138. Don't Become Married to a Particular Project or Idea

EVEN WHEN YOU'RE absolutely certain your way is best, listen to what others have to say. In today's business environment, everything is subject to change. It's easy to become married to a particular project, idea, or method, but don't allow yourself to be inflexible. You never know how others' ideas and yours can be combined, causing something great to evolve. Remain open to other approaches.

Don't resist change because you're stuck in the old way of doing things. A stodgy reputation diminishes your chances for promotion, because managers must lead into the future. People who reject new pathways are simply not good management material.

In addition, resistance to change probably does damage to your firm. Remember that the face of customer needs and expectations changes so rapidly that just sitting still is equivalent to moving backward.

Finally, be open to other people's ideas, and you will find that they reciprocate by opening to yours. Conversely, if you persist in avoiding innovative projects and ideas, you may find a lack of acceptance toward yours.

139. See the Forest Through the Trees

WHILE DETAILS ARE obviously important, some people get so wrapped up in little details that they get sidetracked and lose sight of the big picture. As the expression goes, they can't see the forest through the trees.

This is most commonplace on committees. A group of people begin to haggle over a specific detail, and before long the conversation is hung up on a minute point that isn't even pertinent. Consequently, considerable time is wasted while nothing is accomplished. To avoid this situation, a committee chairperson must follow an agenda and communicate the committee's objective to all members at the start of the meeting.

And just as a committee needs an objective to keep it from getting sidetracked, so must you have a specific goal when working on a particular project. Otherwise, small, insignificant details will distract you, spinning you off in many different directions. Such diversions can throw you off course and derail you before you reach your destination.

SEE ALSO #87.

140. Don't Steal the Limelight from Your Boss

....

ALL GREAT SUPPORTING actors know not to steal the limelight from the star on center stage. Likewise, you must play a similar role with your boss. Think about it: nobody likes to be upstaged, and your boss is no different. Even if you have a low-key boss who seems mellow and laid-back, don't fool yourself. Such a person still relishes being the center of attention now and then. Like everyone else, his ego occasionally needs stroking, so when he's in the limelight let him enjoy it.

When someone is being praised, it's not only bad etiquette to steal his thunder, it's a sign of insecurity. Such poor manners signal others (especially, in this case, your boss) that you desperately want attention and are willing to steal it from someone who deserves it. This is definitely not the image that leads to advancement.

141. Maintain a Sense of Humor

LIGHTEN UP! A sense of humor is a wonderful asset in the workplace. Find ways to take advantage of it rather than trying to deny it, thinking it's not appropriate in the world of business.

A sense of humor keeps your work in proper perspective. When you can see the light side of a serious problem, you approach it more clearly. After all, most difficulties are not as forbidding as they first appear. This attitude sidetracks stress so you can tackle problems head-on.

Humor can be an antidote to stress. When you laugh, certain physiological changes take place that medical experts claim are beneficial—so it should lighten tension in the workplace.

During tense situations, humor can break the ice. A light comment at the start of a negotiation or the beginning of an important meeting tends to relax people. The friendly, non-threatening gesture of humor is always well-received. Notice that speakers use icebreakers to warm up an audience—relating a funny story causes the audience to identify with her.

However, there's a thin line between being funny and offensive. If you think there's the slimmest chance you'll offend someone, keep your mouth shut. Be particularly sensitive about telling jokes that are not politically correct. Even though you make a remark in jest, it may not come across that way to someone else. Don't risk insulting someone—no laugh is worth taking that chance.

Some people have a better sense of humor than others. If your boss is a laid-back person who enjoys a good laugh, having a sense of humor will work in your favor. But if you happen to work for a boss who is humorless, be careful that you don't overdo it. Some people don't think humor is appropiate in the workplace—and if your boss is one of them, you have no choice but to respect his feelings. Otherwise, you'll risk offending him.

142. Never Undersell Yourself

IF YOU BELIEVE in yourself, you can expect others to, because people see you as you see yourself. But if you lack faith in yourself, others tend not to have confidence in you either. Whether it's positive or negative, people will mirror your self-image. Therefore, high self-esteem is essential to your long-term success.

Learn to be your own best salesperson. There's nobody who can sell you as well as you do, nor is there anyone else who has as much incentive to do so. Don't be shy about being your own PR person. When you do an outstanding job on something, it's perfectly permissible to toot your own horn. America's biggest corporations have PR departments, and some even hire outside firms to announce their accomplishments to the world. Celebrities like entertainers and politicians employ such firms, too. If it makes sense for them to promote themselves, it also makes sense for you to promote yourself within your company, and specifically to your boss.

Humility may be a virtue, but too much of it can be self-defeating. Sometimes no one else in the company will broadcast your achievements to your boss. Just don't let your good work consistently go unnoticed. While your modesty may be admirable, it won't get you the credit you deserve. Keep this in mind when you receive a compliment or praise. If you warrant it, gracefully accept it.

143. Never Oversell Yourself

JUST AS YOU SHOULD never undersell yourself, neither should you oversell yourself. Admittedly, the difficulty is in knowing where one stops and the other begins, so you walk a thin line balancing the two.

While you want your achievements to be known to your boss, you don't want to come across as a braggart. So subtlety is the key when broadcasting how wonderful you are. A word of caution: what you think is subtle may not appear subtle to someone else. If you come across as too boastful, you could even disenchant people you have previously won over.

Overselling your capabilities to your boss brings with it the danger that you'll convince her you can do a job that is in reality over your head. Overselling sets you up for failure when you cannot deliver what you have promised.

Rather than oversell yourself, give your boss an honest appraisal of not only your abilities, but your limitations as well. Then your boss can be a better judge of which projects to assign you.

144. Go the Extra Mile

A SIGN ON A CASH register read, "If you don't believe the dead come back to life, you should be here at quitting time." This may appeal to some people's sense of humor, but it's no laughing matter to your boss, who knows that the sign's message is a true representation of people on his payroll, past and present. It's a sad but true commentary on the American workforce, but most people simply go through the motions at work.

It's unfortunate, but an "It's not my job" attitude prevails in today's workplace. There are scores of people who do only what they have to do to keep their jobs, and little more.

If you want to stand above the crowd, demonstrate to your boss that you are always willing to go that extra mile. Prove by your actions that he can depend on you to do more than your share. Become known for your willingness to exert extra effort above and beyond the call of duty. Earn the reputation that you'll bend over backward for the company and its customers, even if you have to work overtime to do it.

In today's competitive workplace, it's not enough to do what's outlined in your job description. That's what you're expected to do, and your paycheck is based on doing just that. To become a highly valued employee, you must make yourself known around the company as a person who gives 100 percent effort every time you step up to the plate. And be the kind of player who, once on base, is going to hustle to score. Become known as a person who refuses to quit and goes all out to avoid letting down the team.

SEE ALSO #56.

145. Don't Take Yourself Too Seriously

It has been said, "A man will do well in commerce as long as he does not believe that his own body odor is perfume." Some people get so caught up in their own self-importance that they turn off everyone around them. They may not even realize that others are poking fun at them behind their backs. Leaving themselves open to such ridicule renders their leadership ineffective. Their willingness to remain out of touch means subordinates soon write them off as unapproachable. Their arrogant attitude makes them inferior communicators.

Each time you're promoted, you'll get respect from people by demonstrating that your down-to-earth qualities remain intact. Putting on airs doesn't make you more important; in fact, the reverse is true. People who take themselves too seriously are viewed as individuals who don't know how to handle success. Their awkwardness in handling it makes them seem unsure whether they deserve to succeed. And one thing is for sure—they won't impress the boss with their sense of self-importance.

Of course, there's a big difference between taking your work seriously and taking yourself seriously. Always take your job seriously. But *you're* another matter—regardless of how important your job is, it's best to take yourself lightly.

146. Ask for Help

NEVER BE TOO PROUD to ask for help. But from whom? Ask anyone you think can help you. Don't be too proud to ask your boss or another senior manager. And likewise, don't let pride stop you from asking a subordinate.

Some people consider it a sign of weakness to ask an underling for help. However, any person who can help you is the right individual to ask. Don't allow biases such as age or position to influence you. When you need help, put your pride aside and get it.

People too uppity to request assistance from a subordinate are making a big mistake. In fact, sometimes a lower-level worker is the ideal person to assist you if your problem lies in his area of expertise. Smart plant managers recognize this and take their questions directly to the person—perhaps someone on the assembly line—who performs a particular function eight hours a day. Seek out the person who has the most expertise in the area of your concern.

When you ask a subordinate for help, chances are he'll be flattered, and you'll do wonders for his morale. This is all the more reason to ask for his help. Don't allow your ego to get in the way. Go ahead and ask, make someone's day!

147. Don't Rely on Intuition Unless You're Absolutely Positive You're Right

MANY OF OUR decisions can be made only through intuition. It doesn't matter how many facts we analyze—when it's crunch time and we must make an important decision, a judgment call may be in order. Is this a reliable decision-making method, particularly when matters of great concern are at stake? The answer to this question is: *it depends*. Some people's intuition historically has proven to be so accurate, they'd be foolish not to trust it. Others whose hunches are right only some of the time would be taking a calculated risk. Therefore, your decision should rest on what and how much is at stake.

From time to time, we all make decisions based on intuition. For example, we judge people by our first impression, and frequently this gut reaction proves to be right. We may use it to determine which products to buy from which companies. Often we choose our careers and the companies to work for based on our intuition. Do we always make the right decisions? No—sometimes we do, and sometimes we don't.

But exactly what is intuition? Is it something we're born with, as some people claim, or do we acquire more of it as we get older? Supposedly, we're born with intuition, but it also seems to be a quality that develops as we're exposed to more experiences. Everything we experience—both good and bad—is stored in our subconscious mind, much the same way that data is stored in a computer. And like a computer, we become programmed over time. Eventually, a little voice in our subconscious tells us, "Do this. It's the right thing to do," and, "Don't do that. It's not going to work."

How much you rely on that little voice shows how much of a risk taker you are. It's one thing to take risks in your personal life or in your own business, but when you work for someone else, you have to use more caution. So in pleasing your boss, rely on your intuition only in circumstances when you're absolutely positive you're right. You'll recognize these moments, and when you do, go with your gut feelings. When you're not so sure, let your boss use her intuition!

148. Delegate

ANYONE WHO HOLDS a position in management must learn to delegate to others. Managers at all levels require this basic skill. To the novice, particularly an individual holding her first managerial position, this is easier said than done. Before others began to report to her, she did everything herself, so making the transition takes some adjusting.

Even if you don't hold a management position, there are times when you must delegate. A secretary, for instance, may be burdened with a heavy workload when his boss lays a high-priority rush job on him. He may have to then lay some of his other assignments on another secretary. He might even farm out some of his remaining duties to other clerical workers—typing, copying, transcribing, and so on.

In upper levels of management, delegation is imperative. It's a matter of time management and economics. By properly delegating to others, your time is freed to devote to high-priority tasks. And if your time is worth more than a subordinate's, it makes good economic sense for him to do a lesser assignment while you work at something that requires your higher skills. For example, a $100-per-hour manager shouldn't be typing his own letters when he has a $10-per-hour secretary.

A word of caution: when you delegate work to others, their performance reflects on you. If they botch up a project, you'll be held directly responsible for those deficiencies. So remember, in the eyes of your boss, their poor performance is viewed as *your* poor performance. Conversely, when they perform well, it's a reflection of your good work. With this in mind, surround yourself with good people. They can make you or break you. Your future rests in their hands.

149. Don't Shoot the Messenger—Reward Him for Bad News

You can't be in your office, in the plant, and out in the field with customers at the same time. It's impossible! For this reason, when you can't be there to observe firsthand, you must rely on others to update you on current events. This feedback is vital, so maintain an open door of communication with your coworkers. To keep the information flowing, let it be known throughout your organization that you welcome those who come bearing news, good or bad.

Don't be one of those shouters who reads the riot act to anyone conveying bad news. After all, it's not the messenger's fault! An adverse reaction from you eventually discourages people who must approach you with unpleasant tidings. Once you scare people away, they'll tell you only what you want to hear. When you intimidate someone who is straightforward with you, you cut off a source of vital feedback. Don't wonder, then, why you find yourself surrounded by yes-men!

To be fully informed, it's vital to keep communication channels open. If you're only hearing good news, by the time you know what's broken, it may be too late to fix it. However, if you're approachable when bad news first breaks, you have a better chance of heading off the problem. And when this happens, the amount of bad news you have to report to your boss is minimized. Needless to say, this puts you at a competitive advantage over your coworker who is constantly reporting bad news to the boss.

This is why you must reward the messenger bearing bad news. Let him know you welcome his message. Ask plenty of questions, and confirm the facts backing up what he has told you.

150. Don't Resist Change—Embrace It

WE ALL HAVE a natural tendency to resist change. Our fear of making a wrong decision makes us procrastinate. It's easier to stick with the status quo than risk a wrong decision. The irony is that refusing to accept change is also a decision—and it could be a wrong one!

Don't resist change—embrace it! While this sounds like a contradiction, it's true that nothing is constant but change. Because we live in a world of continual change, those unable to adapt to it are doomed to obscurity. Let's go one step further: learn to *anticipate* change. Wayne Gretzky, considered the greatest hockey player in the sport's history, was once asked what he considered his secret of success. He said, "I skate to where the puck is going to be, not where it has been."

In the world of business, everything is subject to change at an ever-increasing rate. Staff will change, since the life of a corporation is perpetual versus our limited life span. Locations change. Products change. IBM originally manufactured butcher scales; Honda Motor Company started as a motorcycle company; DuPont was the world's largest manufacturer of gunpowder and America's largest supplier from the War of 1812 through World War I; American Express started out as the pony express! Likewise, company names change. IBM was originally called Computing-Tabulating-Recording Company; after being in business for 90 years, Standard Oil Company changed its name in 1972 to Exxon; Avon Products was originally called California Perfume Company.

Notice how top managers are most likely to be individuals who embrace change. Accordingly, they like to surround themselves with flexible people who also welcome change. Conversely, people who resist change are poor candidates to move up the corporate ladder.

151. Develop Your Networking Skills

WHILE WHO YOU know is not as important as what you know, don't underestimate the value of knowing people. Let's take it one step further: who you know is a valuable asset only if you can use your contacts to your advantage. Otherwise, simply knowing the "right" people doesn't mean squat.

Often the day-to-day things going on in corporate America happen through informal channels. Your effectiveness depends on how you interact with people both inside and outside the company, and to a degree, your success depends upon how these people view you. Not only must they like you, they must believe in you. The rapport you establish with them plays an important role in both your present and future career. While it may seem insignificant early in your career, building relationships with many people over a period of time, if done effectively, can evolve into one of your most important assets.

Successful executives develop relationships with hundreds and even thousands of people during the course of their careers. Just where these relationships are developed runs the gamut. Inside networking includes people you meet as you work in different departments and divisions. Then too, there are people you interact with at meetings, in the cafeteria, in the executive dining room, and so on. What's important is that you make many friends throughout the organization over a period of time.

Outside networking includes meeting people at conventions, workshops, and continuing education programs. Then there are customers, personal friends, and other social contacts, as well as the people to whom they introduce you. Outside your own company, you should always network—you meet people while vacationing, parents of your children's friends, fellow travelers on an airplane or subway. The list goes on and on.

In addition to those individuals you meet on an "accidental" basis, you should also purposely seek out people you'd like to get to know because you feel they can advance your career. These sought-out people can be your most valuable sources. Like other contacts, you must stay in constant communication with them.

Once you have a new acquaintance, create a file on him. Keep in the file information about the contact ranging from phone numbers and addresses to other personal data such as birthdays, anniversaries, children's names, and so on. Keep in touch, and in time a relationship will develop.

152. Never Tolerate a Lack of Integrity

In an ideal world, integrity is a given in the workplace. Unfortunately, in the real world, lack of integrity is commonplace. This doesn't mean you should passively accept it. On the contrary, consider it unacceptable behavior.

Integrity starts at the top of an organization. Management leads by example: the virtues of the CEO and senior management permeate the company. When employees and customers are treated fairly, they respond in kind. However, when a company has one-sided policies, its workforce sits up and takes notice. For instance, a company producing a shoddy product that offers a poor value to its customers negatively influences its employees' sense of pride. The same is true when the company makes false claims to its customers or fails to provide proper service or honor its warranty. When the market is poor, senior managers of a publicly owned company are bound to upset stockholders by getting undeserved bonuses and fat stock options. Behavior of this nature sends a mixed message throughout the organization.

Lack of integrity must never be acceptable. As Henry David Thoreau said, "It is true enough said that a corporation has no conscience; but a corporation of conscientious men is a corporation with a conscience." In this context, a corporation managed by unscrupulous managers is a corporation without scruples. Such a lack of integrity must never be tolerated.

In all my years in business, I never met a successful person who didn't respect integrity. I can assure you that your boss will, too. So never compromise your integrity!

153. Never Tolerate Disloyalty

You owe allegiance to the company that pays your wages. Pledge your loyalty to it and never tolerate disloyalty from anyone. Come down hard on anyone who makes a hostile remark about your employer. Don't ignore unfriendly comments; let your feelings be known to those who make them. Be forceful when you express your sentiments. Your failure to speak out in such a circumstance implies consent.

Often, loyal employees don't want to create waves, so they turn a deaf ear to derogatory remarks. Simply put, they avoid conflict by remaining silent. But remaining silent can be a form of disloyalty, so it's better to take a stand and let people know you won't tolerate their infidelity.

Generally speaking, employees who are loyal to their bosses are rewarded in kind by having the loyalty of their bosses. So remember, it's a two-way street. Loyalty begets loyalty.

154. Unclutter Your Cluttered Desk

ISN'T IT INTERESTING that some people who dress immaculately can at the same time work at an unkempt desk? There are two good reasons you shouldn't have a cluttered desk. First, being unorganized wastes time. "It may look unorganized, but I know where everything is," some respond. Well, you may think you can find things on such a desk, but certainly not as efficiently as if it were better organized. Second, you don't want to project a sloppy image to people who visit your office. This is like having important guests drop in unexpectedly at your home, only to find it looking like a pigpen! Like your home, your desk is a reflection of who you are.

It's particularly important to unclutter your desk if you have a boss who's the proud owner of an impeccably neat desk. Generally, bosses who sit behind an orderly desk have little tolerance for subordinates with disorderly desks. In fact, even if your boss's desk looks like it got hit by a cyclone, he may still be annoyed with yours. He may be one of those "Do as I say, not as I do" types, so don't expect your boss to bless your mess!

155. Be Likeable

WHO WOULDN'T KNOW you score more points with your boss, co-workers, and customers when they like you! You'd think being likeable was a given, if it were not for the undeniably high number of disagreeable people in the world.

But when you take a long look around you and observe how many people don't seem likeable, you realize they just don't get it. Too many are unfriendly, nasty, self-serving, self-righteous, arrogant, opinionated—you get the point, they're just not likeable. If there is a congenial side to them, they aren't bringing it to work!

Of course, the same qualities it takes to win friends and influence people off the job apply on the job. It doesn't take much energy to make a conscious effort to be likeable, even if you have to extend yourself. Why, since you're not in a popularity contest, is this so important? Because when people like you, they will go out of their way for you! You can be certain that if you are likeable, your boss will favor you over people who are equally qualified.

156. Don't Be a Creature of Habit

To SOME EXTENT, we're all creatures of habit. Generally, however, the higher you climb the corporate ladder, the more likely it is that your repetitive chores can be performed by a subordinate. But even those of us with influential and creative jobs still occasionally find ourselves handling mundane tasks.

Let's face it, we all have to perform our share of ordinary tasks that require minimal creativity or brainpower. Because we do them with such ease and little thought, they become automatic and, in time, we do them by rote. But you should avoid falling into the trap of being a creature of habit. Look for different ways to improve the efficiency or quality of these routine tasks. Doing so will keep your mind sharp and your performance will improve.

A real estate agent, for example, might take a different route home every day. Not only does this break up the boredom of the drive home, she may come across a desirable property that's been put on the market for the first time. An executive might experiment with different messages to leave on voice mail machines and notice which techniques generate the highest percentage of returned calls. And a manager might explore a variety of techniques to praise subordinates as he searches for new ways to motivate them.

Of course, the more interesting you make your work, the more interesting and creative you will appear to your boss. Conversely, people who are bored by their work give the impression that they themselves are boring.

So the key is to challenge yourself to try different things, always striving to improve and keep your work interesting.

157. Surround Yourself with People Who Reflect the Values of Your Company

WHEN HIRING EMPLOYEES or adding someone from another department to your staff, look for people who reflect the values of the company. While it may be obvious why these people are desirable, few of us make a concentrated effort to seek them out. Be prepared to subject yourself to a tedious, time-consuming process. It will require you to spend many hours conducting in-depth interviews, asking pertinent questions to select the right people. What you will learn about these people via a personal interview won't be revealed on a job application or a resume. Although it's a demanding job, the payback will be a reduction in the turnover that is costly as well as destructive to morale.

When you select people who reflect the values of your company's culture, odds are that they will work in harmony with your existing workforce, because those employees have already bought into the program. Ideally, the new employees should display similar qualities: a strong work ethic, a respect for customers, and a quest for excellence.

SEE ALSO #18, #76, #96, #128, AND #137.

158. Know When to Say No

Somebody once said, "When a diplomat says yes, he means maybe. When he says maybe, he means no. And when he says no, he's no longer a diplomat." In the workplace, although diplomacy is a virtue, you can't beat around the bush like a diplomat can. Often a firm *no* is mandatory, no ifs, ands, or buts.

We have a natural tendency to resist saying no because we want people to like us. In business, however, this is a serious flaw. Sometimes it's necessary to say no—emphatically and without hesitation. Procrastination is a sign of indecisiveness and projects an image of weakness.

The worst-case scenario is what's known as the "slow no," when a person keeps putting off saying no and builds up another's hopes. Leaving people in a holding pattern instead of informing them of the decision up front causes them to waste valuable time spinning their wheels. This is frustrating and exasperating. As you can see, the slow no is far worse than an out-and-out no.

At MRI it is important to get a decision promptly. Whether we ask a client, "Will you make an offer of employment?" or we ask a candidate, "Will you accept an offer?", we welcome a "no" decision almost as much as a "yes." A "maybe" drags the decision out and generally results in a poor final outcome.

It's best to respond with a decisive no and follow it up by clearly stating your reasons. If the other party doesn't concur with your decision, she knows where you stand and has the option of restating her case for you to reconsider.

159. Treat Your Boss Like You Treat Your Best Customer

YOUR BOSS IS YOUR customer, and like every customer, you must understand his needs. With this in mind, recognize that your boss has two distinct needs you must fulfill:

1. Make his work and life easier.

2. Make him look good.

Just like a valued customer, your boss must be "sold" on you, too. He pays for your services and wants to get his money's worth. Of course, the secret is to give him more than he pays for. Do your job so exceedingly well that you convince him there's no place he can find a better value. You are a salesperson with a product to sell—*you!* And, just like any other product, you can't allow yourself to sit on the shelf. Don't rest on your laurels; past performance is history. You must continually make improvements to avoid becoming obsolete.

In a competitive workplace, you can no more take your boss for granted than you can take a customer for granted. You must continually qualify for your job. To accomplish this, constantly go that extra mile, exceeding not only your boss's expectations, but your own. And like a salesperson, you aggressively anticipate your boss's needs and deliver—again and again and again. It's a sales job that never stops.

160. Schedule Appointments with Your Boss

WHEN YOU HAVE an important issue to discuss with your boss, set up a meeting to see her. By doing this, you send three messages to her:

1. What you have to say is not a trivial matter—it's important enough to require a definite time to meet.

2. Both her time and your time are of value to you.

3. You are a professional.

In addition, asking your boss in advance for an appointment is simply a polite thing to do. It sure beats barging in on her unannounced, because it gives her time to reflect on what your meeting entails. If she is allowed to prepare, she's more apt to focus on the merit of what you have to offer. Remember that catching her when she is distracted by other issues places you at a definite disadvantage.

Bear in mind that to ask for your boss's undivided attention, you must have a critical need. Frivolous or frequent appointments will only annoy her and dilute your impact.

161. Take Ownership

You don't have to own a piece of the business to feel owner-ship. For example, as a citizen of the United States, you have ownership of your country even if you don't own land. Likewise, as an employee you have a stake in the company comparable to that of a shareholder.

Certainly, you have a vested interest in the well-being and prosperity of the company that employs you. The future of you and your family depends on it. So you should pull for its success, doing your best to help achieve its objectives.

Too often, workers simply go through the motions of their jobs, doing only enough to get by. This disenfranchised attitude telegraphs to their coworkers and boss that they are driven only by their paychecks. Apathy is not only a drain on morale, it is self-destructive.

Take pride in your work as well as your company. Exhibit-ing this form of company ownership is certain to score points with your boss.

162. Inform Your Boss About Your Career Plan

DID YOU EVER NOTICE how deliberately people plan their vacations? Every detail is contemplated in advance and with such enthusiasm. If they'd only give as much thought to planning their careers the same way!

You should have an intermediate career plan (3 to 5 years) and a long-range one (10 to 20 years). Put it in writing so that you clearly know where you want to be, and refer to it frequently.

And don't keep it a secret. Discuss it with your boss and seek his advice. Chances are, he will admire your ambition, encourage you, and advise you on how to achieve your objectives. Approach him periodically for feedback on how to stay on your career path. Ask for his evaluation of your progress. The more you involve him, the more likely he'll support you.

163. Don't Be a Prima Donna

WE READ ABOUT them in the sports pages and entertainment sections of our newspapers—the superathletes and famous actors who insist on being placed on a pedestal. We have a tendency to stereotype certain types of creative people such as artists, writers, and interior decorators as temperamental. And because they're creative, we sometimes let them get away with it.

In truth, however, nobody has the right to behave poorly, as if they're so special people will accept their crass conduct. It's bad enough that we're exposed to prima donnas in sports and the arts. But it doesn't stop there. They also exist in corporate America.

You know the type. The top salesperson who outproduces the rest of the force and feels this entitles him to preferential treatment (bigger commission, better car, plusher office). Then there's the bully attorney, the snooty art director, the budding executive with a supercilious tone of voice.

Prima donnas aren't shy about making demands of the boss, even pressing her to bend company policy their way. And, for a time, they may get what they demand. But there's always another player just around the corner who performs as well or better, who also puts the team first. A boss will bide her time until such a player arrives to bring these nonplayers down to earth—or to boot them out the door!

164. Be Generous with the Gifts You Give Your Boss

EVERYONE LIKES RECEIVING gifts, and so does your boss. Just as you'd remember a good friend's birthday, don't overlook your boss on special occasions simply because you work for her. Some people seem to think it's OK to exclude the head honcho, but they're mistaken.

Excluding your boss from your Christmas shopping list when you give gifts to everyone else may be hurtful to her. Yet it happens every Christmas season.

Remember, it's a two-way street. Be especially sure to reciprocate if your boss gives you birthday and holiday gifts. Consider it a simple courtesy. In this case, treat your boss the same way you'd treat a coworker or a friend.

A creative selection is bound to make a favorable impression. Buy something that's personal—but not too personal. Choose something related to your boss's hobbies, such as golf, photography, or cooking. This shows you put some time and effort into what you bought. A good hobby-related book or one about business or current affairs is also a good choice, and books are affordable. (You needn't spend excessively to be in good taste.)

You might also purchase something durable and useful, such as a gold pen or gold key chain. A gift of this nature will remind your boss daily that you are considerate and thoughtful.

Use discretion in your gift selection. Generally, clothing items involve complex issues of size, color, and personal preference. And much too personal are items for use in the bathroom or bedroom.

165. Never Underestimate the Power of the Grapevine

In both large and small companies, rumors abound. Often what you hear is nothing more than hearsay. For example, a secretary might hear her boss say something on the telephone and, because she hears only part of the conversation, misinterprets it. She repeats it to a coworker, who repeats it to another coworker, and so on. By the time it goes through the rumor mill, it hardly resembles the truth.

Other rumors begin in the lunchroom when someone overhears a conversation from another table. Or workers overhear conversations from another cubicle or the open door of a coworker's office. Some rumors are the result of idle gossip, when one person speculates on what he thinks might be fact and a second party accepts it as fact. Many sources are unreliable.

Then too, some stories heard on the grapevine are indeed quite accurate. Information may leak after an important document is left in a copying machine, a memo is placed face-up on someone's desk, or somebody with a big mouth simply discloses some confidential information. Still another reliable source are rumors based on observations from people at the bottom of an organization. For instance, before a plant closes, workers on the assembly line might observe the telltale signs of shoddy workmanship, poor maintenance of machinery, or inferior quality of materials. Being exposed to the day-to-day operations signals to them that the plant is poorly managed, and because it's operating in the red, it will soon be closed. In such an instance, they can anticipate what will ultimately happen before upper management has the slightest clue. Keep in mind, too, that where there is smoke, there usually is fire.

166. Block Out Irrelevant Remarks and Concentrate on What's Important

DID YOU EVER notice how some extraordinary executives focus only on relevant issues, blocking out nonessential, extraneous ones? For instance, when a subordinate talks somewhat incoherently, mixing jibber-jabber with fact, a skillful executive stays focused on main issues, always keeping the conversation on course. Such managers excel at zeroing in on what's essential and weeding out the inconsequential. This valuable people skill can cut down on unnecessary, time-consuming small talk. People who lack this craft often find themselves engaged in hurried, long-winded, or confused conversation.

This same skill can be useful in conducting committee meetings. By sticking to important matters, you avoid bogging down your meeting with frivolous topics. We've all experienced the frustration that goes with serving on a committee that lacks direction. It drifts and nothing gets done. It's this kind of meeting that is referred to when someone remarks that a camel was obviously designed by a committee!

167. Avoid Awkward Food When Dining Out

A MEAL WITH your boss can leave a positive or negative impression, depending on how you manage your food. While most people don't give it a second thought, certain foods can cause you to lose your poise at the table. Common sense dictates that it's foolish to risk looking like a slob to your boss just to satisfy a temporary craving.

For example, it's difficult to wolf down a dish of spaghetti without flipping a spot onto your shirt. And forget about ordering a giant sandwich that you have to hold with two hands—if it's wider than your mouth, you don't want to eat it in front of your boss. It doesn't matter that the restaurant you're at has one of the world's greatest burgers—don't order it unless you intend to eat it with a knife and fork.

Even ordering soup can be a problem. You may not be aware that you slurp, but if you do, it will not go unnoticed by your boss. Likewise, certain finger foods like juicy gyros and crumbling tacos are not advisable.

In general, when it's a part of doing business, you simply want to avoid being a conspicuous diner. If you're attending a banquet where everyone has corn on the cob, it's understood that you'll all be dealing with the same food in the same way. And if the agenda says "ribs night" and everyone is wearing a bib, by all means join in. Such an event encourages a group to loosen up, and temporary lapses of dining etiquette are excused.

168. Don't Allow Failure to Defeat You

IT'S COMMONLY KNOWN that those who never fail are people who don't take risks. Thus, it can be said that risk takers have had their share of failures along the way. In general, those who take the greatest risk reap the greatest reward. The secret to success is accepting failure without succumbing.

Did you know that Babe Ruth, who hit 714 home runs, at one time held the record for the most strikeouts? He struck out 1,330 times! Nobody likes failure, but successful individuals understand that it's part of the game—so they accept it, regroup, and calculate new and better ways to succeed. High achievers fail many times before they ultimately win. Conversely, people who never succeed fail simply because they gave up too soon.

Also note that successful people don't buckle under criticism. Occasionally criticism contains kernels of wisdom to be gleaned. Other times it may be untrue or even unkind. But winners don't allow it to discourage them. They have conviction in what they do and believe in themselves. They may even use criticism to spur them on, knowing that success may be just around the corner!

Those who succeed have learned to use rejection in a constructive way. Instead of saying, "he doesn't like me," they say, "he doesn't like my ideas."

Some of the world's most creative people faced rejection:

- "I'm sorry, Mr. Kipling, but you just don't know how to use the English language."—*San Francisco Examiner* in 1889 to Rudyard Kipling

- "Sure-fire rubbish."—*New York Herald Tribune's* 1935 review of George and Ira Gershwin's *Porgy and Bess*

- "This book is for the season only."—*New York Herald Tribune*'s review of *The Great Gatsby* by F. Scott Fitzgerald

- "The Beatles? They are on the wane."—The Duke of Edinburgh, 1966

Imagine the world's loss if these artists had allowed criticism to defeat them. Learn this lesson: when you fail an assignment, miss a promotion, or get turned down in any way, accept it as a passage, not as a role. Learn from it, and press on. You can experience failure without becoming one.

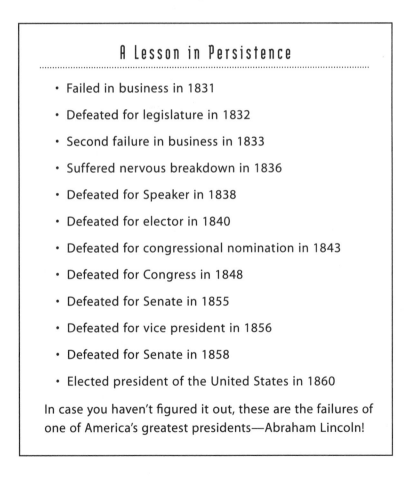

A Lesson in Persistence

- Failed in business in 1831

- Defeated for legislature in 1832

- Second failure in business in 1833

- Suffered nervous breakdown in 1836

- Defeated for Speaker in 1838

- Defeated for elector in 1840

- Defeated for congressional nomination in 1843

- Defeated for Congress in 1848

- Defeated for Senate in 1855

- Defeated for vice president in 1856

- Defeated for Senate in 1858

- Elected president of the United States in 1860

In case you haven't figured it out, these are the failures of one of America's greatest presidents—Abraham Lincoln!

169. Go for the Bottom Line

THE PHRASE "the bottom line" is heard so much in everyday conversation, it's become a cliché. Still, it's worth mentioning, because a business without profits is destined to become an endangered species. In the world of business, profit is not a dirty word. A company must make money in order to grow and prosper.

This doesn't mean that the bottom line is the all-inclusive reason a business exists. Its number one priority should not always be its shareholders. In addition to shareholders, there are other stakeholders, including employees, customers, and suppliers, as well as the community where it resides.

Still, without a healthy bottom line, a company cannot serve any of its stakeholders for long. When the red ink flows, a company loses its capacity to employ and promote its employees. Its competitive edge is lost, which encumbers its capacity to provide value and service to its customers. Likewise, a company with heavy losses is unable to contribute substantially to the community.

So, for good reason, senior management must always have an eye on its bottom line. It knows well the necessity of operating in the black. You, too, must make a concentrated effort to perform your job with a bottom-line mentality. With this mind-set, you'll be able to focus on things that contribute to the bottom line, eliminating functions that do not. By doing so, you are certain to be a valued employee. This will also score you many well-deserved points with your boss.

Index